Don't Quit Your Day Job

An Educator's Guide to Student Engagement

Aaron Daffern

Library of Congress Control Number: 2018902241

Copyright © 2018 David Aaron Daffern

All rights reserved. This book or any portion thereof may not be reproduced or used in any manner whatsoever without the express written permission of the author except for the use of brief quotations in a book review or scholarly journal.

First Printing: 2018

ISBN-13: 978-0-9990241-3-3

Aaron Daffern Consulting

www.AaronDaffern.com

DEDICATION

To the educators in the trenches.
You toil daily for the lives of your students, sometimes giving them the only chance they'll have in life.

Never stop fighting.

CONTENTS

	Introduction	1
1	The Need for Engagement	3
2	The Missing Piece	9
3	Degrees of Learning	15
4	Motivational Theories	21
5	CRAVE Learning	27
6	The Power of Self-Beliefs	33
7	Self-Beliefs Predict Success	39
8	Causes for Success or Failure	45
9	Growth Mindset	51
10	Influencing Competence Beliefs	57
11	Character by Osmosis	63
12	Relationships Develop Self-Esteem	69
13	Students Watch Teacher Interactions	75
14	Relationships Increase Achievement	81
15	Relationships Help At-Risk Students	87
16	Keys for Intrinsic Motivation	93
17	Persistence and Regulation	99
18	Autonomy Fuels Creativity	105
19	Structure Supports Autonomy	111
20	Control Kills Autonomy	119

21	Value Matters	125
22	Mastery Goal Orientation	131
23	Teachers Influence Goal Orientation	137
24	Performance Goal Orientation	143
25	Different Performance Goals	149
26	Developing Interest	155
27	Sustained Interest	161
28	Emotions Matter	167
29	Emotions Affect Creativity	173
30	Negative Emotions Harm Learning	179
	Afterward	185
Appendix 1	CRAVE Review of Literature	187
Appendix 2	CRAVE Inventory	203
Appendix 3	Learning Style Inventory	207

INTRODUCTION

For many educators, the joy of teaching was lost long ago. What began as a wonderful, life-changing adventure has, for some, become a relentless grind. Every year I see quality teachers beat down by the system and leave the profession. My hope is that rather than quitting their day jobs, teachers will take a fresh look at their classrooms. I truly believe that the solution for many teachers is to increase student engagement. When students take on the burden of intellectual discovery, the possibilities are endless. Effective learning is done *by* students, not *to* students.

Teaching should be fun, not futile.

This book is intended to guide educators on a reflective, thirty-day journey. Grounded in over thirty years of educational and psychological research, teachers will find practical applications built on a solid theoretical foundation. When cited, references are included at the end of each chapter. A comprehensive review of literature encompassing the entirety of this book's scholarly underpinnings can be found in Appendix 1.

Divided into thirty daily segments, the chapters are grouped into six equal sets of five. Days 1-5 look at the need for engaging students and the relevant literature on the topic. Days 6-10 begin looking at the first of five facets of student motivation. The last four groups of five (e.g., Days 11-15, 16-20, etc.) explore the remaining four facets.

If you'd like to transform your teaching in a month, you can read a chapter each day and have a completely different view of the needs of your students by the beginning of the following month. Alternately, you can take a more measured approach and read a chapter each weekday. Within six weeks, you will have a new appreciation of how to engage all students.

Starting at Day 6, the last section of each chapter briefly overviews a teaching technique or classroom structure that targets student motivation. Following each chapter, you'll find a question and an action. To make the most of your effort, take time each day to respond to the question in the space provided. Reflect on the day's reading, evaluate your own teaching situation, and consider implementing the suggested action to increase engagement.

Day 1: The Need For Engagement

I couldn't figure out why the TV remote wasn't working. All I wanted to do was watch the news before I left the house but now I had a bigger crisis. One of my children had probably messed with the remote. Even worse, the TV might be broken! I stood in front of my darkened television uselessly mashing the power button on the remote. If tenacity and sheer stubbornness could have solved the problem, the matter would have ended there. However, that plan wasn't getting anywhere.

Working through the many possible causes of my dilemma, I began to apply my (self-acknowledged) intellectual prowess to the matter at hand. I tried positioning myself directly in front of the sensor, thinking that perhaps an object might be obstructing the infrared beam. When that didn't work, I took a cleaning cloth and carefully wiped down the diode at the end of the remote and the plastic covering the receptor on the television unit. Stray fingerprints, it seems, only show up on car windows the day after I clean them.

The remote was not the original one that came with the television but instead was a universal remote replacement. I next began to suspect that the remote had somehow become uncalibrated for my Sony television. Pulling out the remote's instructions, which I had miraculously found in the kitchen junk drawer, I ran through the sequence needed to configure the remote. I held down the setup button for three seconds until the red light on the remote stayed on. Then, I punched in the 4-digit sequence designed to work with Sony televisions. A satisfying double blink of the red light let me know that the remote was now correctly configured. With a flourish I made solid tactile contact with the power button.

Yet nothing happened.

Obsessed

At this point I became obsessed with finding the solution. Forgetting all about the news I intended to watch or even the errand I was about to run, I took the malfunctioning technology as a personal challenge. Having run through all the logical possibilities, my mind began to frantically work through seemingly ridiculous solutions. I tried spinning around three times with the remote. Next I hid behind the couch and popped up to zap the TV as if I were a Doughboy peering over the trench into No Man's Land. Weirder things have worked before, trust me. I even closed my eyes and pushed random sequences of buttons in sheer desperation.

Heather, my wife, found me a few moments later balanced on one foot. I was aiming the remote through my legs with my back to the television, muttering something like a Gregorian chant. "What are you doing?" she asked, alarmed at my strange behavior. She knew I could be a bit obsessive about certain things but she'd never seen me like this before. Or at least recently.

"What does it look like I'm doing?!?" I strongly intoned with a manic look in my eyes (I don't yell at my wife). With sweat streaking down my forehead, my shirt plastered to my back, I grunted, "The remote isn't working! I can't figure out why!"

It took everything within Heather to not bark out a laugh. She slowly walked over to the wall and stooped down. "I'm sorry, Aaron, it's my fault. I unplugged the TV when I vacuumed the living room earlier and I guess I forgot to plug it back in." She left me standing there with a haunted look in my eyes, staring at the remote as if it were an alien object.

Teaching and Learning

When this happened to me a few years ago, I quickly moved on from it. I didn't think of it again until I recently began to ponder the mysteries of teaching. Education is not easy, my friends. If teaching were as uncomplicated as telling students what they needed to learn and do, life would be ridiculously simple. Because students aren't file folders into which teachers can drop knowledge, instruction and learning must take place.

I list those two elements - instruction and learning - separately on purpose. While some may believe the two terms to be synonymous, experience has taught me otherwise. Instruction is what I do as a teacher. For the most part, I control what I say, what books we'll use, and what assignments my students will complete.

Learning, on the other hand, relies on the students. At the end of the day, it doesn't matter what I say or do. Only what the students actually learn makes a difference. While I cannot control what students learn, my job as an instructor is to heavily influence it. My role is to act as a learning guide and facilitator, helping students acquire the necessary knowledge and skills for a successful life.

Need for Engagement

It was as I was remembering the TV episode in the context of education that an epiphany struck. You see, learning in my classroom had been somewhat fickle up to that point. While I tried my hardest to use best practices, hone my craft, and select rigorous yet appropriate tasks, sometimes my lessons bombed. For no apparent reason, my students would zone out in spite of all the hard work I'd done to prepare. Other times, I would throw something together on the fly. Because of a fire drill or last-minute assembly, my well-laid plans would be useless and I'd have to scramble. For whatever reason, however, those lessons sometimes worked. The students couldn't get enough and they learned in leaps and bounds.

Teaching and learning work together but are not the same. For the most part, learning is proportional to the quality of instruction. However, there is something else at play. My experiences with highly-variable lesson effectiveness showed me that there was a hidden factor. Something other than my instructional prowess contributed to students' learning. Until I figured out what that was and worked on affecting it, my instruction would be subject to unseen forces.

Then I remembered my incident with the TV remote. In a sudden moment of clarity, the puzzle pieces fit together perfectly. Learning depended on more than what I did with my "remote" in front of the classroom. Trying to punch in the right sequences of buttons to make learning occur only worked if the students were plugged in. When students weren't engaged, learning didn't happen.

Solid instructional practices are all well and good but mean nothing without student engagement.

Day 1

Question: In your experience, what engages students in learning?

_____
_____
_____
_____
_____
_____
_____
_____
_____
_____
_____
_____

Action: Find a teaching partner to join you on this journey. Having an accountability partner will give you someone to share your ideas with. It will also encourage you to keep reading and try some new ideas.

Day 2: The Missing Piece

Learning happens when instructional techniques meet student needs.

Usually.

Students grow in knowledge when proven, research-based practices are employed by teachers.

For the most part.

Experience, research, and common sense, however, have shown me that teaching and learning are not always correlated. Improving one will usually improve the other.

But it isn't guaranteed.

The missing piece in the learning equation is engagement. For students to truly learn something, *they* have to do the work. They have to create knowledge. Their brains need to connect their existing schema to the new information. Learning is done *by* the student, not *to* the student.

Classroom Observations

When I first became a principal, I dedicated myself to improving the learning in my school. Seeing as how school effectiveness revolved around student growth, I set out to be a presence in the classrooms. I vowed not to be a desk-bound principal, ruling my domain through passive-aggressive group emails. No, I determined to be a top-rate instructional leader. I made it a point to be in classrooms on a consistent basis, helping teachers become more proficient in their craft.

I quickly found, however, that watching the teachers didn't give me enough information. For the most part, my teachers were more than adequate. They presented information in a logical sequence. Their classroom management seemed alright and they followed the district curriculum. But for everything that was the same, the results were completely different.

Some parents couldn't say enough nice things about their student's teachers. Others emailed me to try and have their child moved to another class. Scores on benchmarks and state tests also showed that a vast gulf existed between effective teachers and those that were barely hanging on. When I couldn't find the difference by watching the teachers, I changed the focus of my observations.

I began to observe the students.

Lightbulbs

What I saw when I began to study the students blew my mind. In some classes, an energetic hum of curiosity filled the room. Students worked together, asked questions, and made connections. The stereotypical image of a light bulb going off over students' heads seemed to actually be happening. The students fully engaged in learning and their thirst for knowledge seemed contagious.

Then I saw the other classrooms. While the instruction was similar, the level of student involvement differed greatly. Students in these classrooms went through the motions. They obeyed the teacher, listened intently, and turned in their assignments. Theoretically, they were learning the same things as their more successful counterparts. Yet the evidence pointed to a great difference between the two types of classrooms.

Both classrooms witnessed solid teaching strategies. In the first, more exciting classrooms, students actively engaged in the lessons. The other classrooms saw students sitting-and-getting, listening passively to the teacher. In the first, students worked to generate meaning from new information. In the second, students memorized information to regurgitate for final exams.

Engagement

My attention had been on the wrong participant in learning. If I wanted to help my school become more effective, I saw that I needed to focus on the students, not the teachers, when observing classrooms. What they did during a lesson would be much more informational that what the teacher was doing. Two teachers could give the exact same lesson with the same strategies and materials yet bear different results.

Working on the process of elimination, I reasoned that something else was at work in the learning process. Trying to yield student achievement from substandard teaching is like getting blood from a turnip. Yet instruction wasn't the only factor. It was the response of the students, I finally saw, that completed the equation.

Learning was the result of engagement. When students energetically participated in learning, when they knowingly and willfully interact with information, great things happen. Yet what caused student engagement?

Student Motivation

Good teaching can influence engagement. Some lessons are naturally fun. Some activities generate interest and excitement. Other techniques tend to put children into an educationally-induced coma. Yet to lay the entire responsibility at the feet of instructional choices seemed insufficient. How could student engagement not include students themselves?

It finally dawned on me that the missing piece was student motivation.

Students come to school with their own desires and goals. Sometimes overt, sometimes unconscious, I'd seen many lessons derailed by simple student apathy. There is nothing more frightening in a classroom than student indifference.

If students aren't motivated to learn, engagement won't happen.

If teachers don't make wise instructional decisions, engagement won't happen.

When there is no student engagement, learning is out of the picture.

The magic happens when the two factors intermix. Solid teaching plus motivated students make learning a possibility.

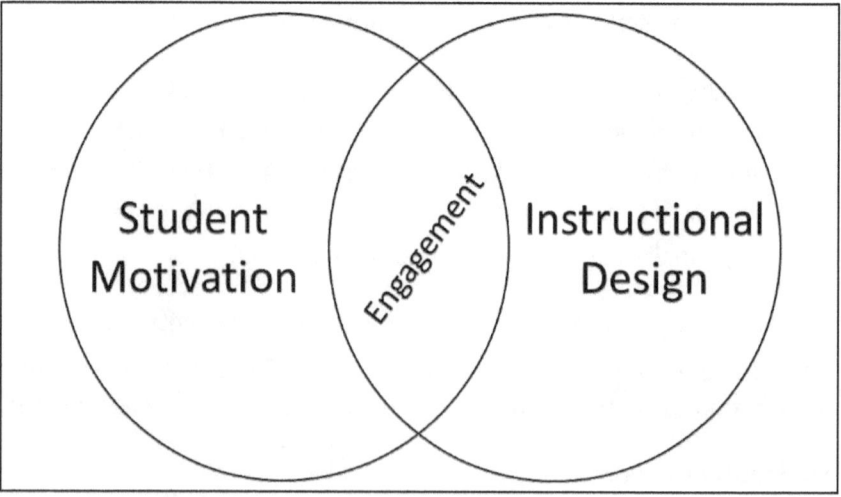

Figure 1: Engagement Venn Diagram

The Missing Piece

The factor that I seemed to be missing in the equation was student motivation. While my education, experience, and certification taught me what good instructional design looked like, I couldn't quite put my finger on student motivation. What was it that made students tick? What did they want from the classroom?

Should teachers provide structure and order so students always know what was expected of them? Should they instead focus on relating to the students and making learning personal? Were tangible rewards the answer or did students respond more to a competitive atmosphere? Should classrooms mainly focus on making learning fun?

While finding the missing piece to the learning puzzle, I realized that I didn't even know how to begin to answer my questions. Instead of relying on my experiences as an educator, I wanted to know what research had to say about student motivation. Surely someone, somewhere, within the last 40 years had figured out what motivates students to learn. If I could just figure out which buttons to push, I could help my teachers design instruction to motivate every student.

Day 2

Question: When you learn something new, what motivates you to keep going when you encounter setbacks?

_____
_____
_____
_____
_____
_____
_____
_____
_____
_____
_____
_____

Action: Identify a student you currently have or have taught recently as a target student. Make understanding him/her a primary focus for transforming your teaching. When asked to incorporate a lesson idea or teaching tip, keep your target student in mind. Your goal is to better engage him/her in your instruction.

Day 3: Degrees of Learning

As I began to search for answers to the student motivation conundrum, I came across an interesting research study conducted by Carl Benware and Edward Deci over 30 years ago. They sought to study the motivational mindsets of students who were given a task for different reasons. Half of the students, the control group, received information with the purpose of learning it for a test. The other half, the variable group, were given the same information to study but with a caveat. Their purpose was to study the material in order to teach it to another student. That other student, whose only access to the material would be through a member of the variable group, would then take a test.

The question they wanted to study was simple. Did changing the purpose for learning something (i.e., taking a test vs teaching someone else) change the level and quality of learning?

They hoped to induce a more intrinsically-motivated, active learning mindset in the variable group. They reasoned that learning something to teach someone else would cause those learners to process information more conceptually. To teach something successfully, one must truly understand it. Simply memorizing random, disjointed facts might work when completing a multiple-choice test but it wouldn't help students tutor someone else over the content.

Though not the primary purpose of the article, those two types of learning, active and passive, stuck out in my mind. Still in the infancy of my search for answers to the student engagement dilemma, I had not yet thought about different types of learning. To me, learning was learning. Yet, what I came to find out was that there were many levels of learning.

Results

Both the control group and variable group ended up taking the test over the material. For the control group, that was expected. For the variable group, however, the researchers pulled a fast one on them. They told the variable group students that before they taught the information to the new students, they themselves would take a test over the material. The researchers said they wanted to discover how much of the material the variable group students learned before they taught it to someone else. After the test, they were told that they actually wouldn't be teaching the material to another student. They learned the purpose of the study was to try and induce an active learning mindset in the variable group, not teach the information to someone else.

The results of the test and a questionnaire showed that the two groups did differ significantly. The variable group expressed more intrinsic motivation, more interest in the material, and more enjoyment of the experiment overall. Most interesting, however, was the difference in the test results. The researchers split the exam into two sections. Both groups performed similarly on the half of the test that measured surface-level, rote learning. Concerning the deeper, conceptual learning half of the test, though, the variable group performed at a much higher level. Whereas the control group got less than half of the conceptual questions correct, the variable group scored better than 75% on that section.

This study helped give form to a truth about learning that previously remained hidden from me. In my search to better understand student motivation and how it impacts engagement and learning, I needed to differentiate between active and passive learning. Within learning itself existed various degrees of effectiveness.

Degrees of Learning

The research study induced a more active learning mindset in the variable group by using a simple ruse. Yet how does that relate to our classrooms today? How does the degree of learning correlate with student motivation? If you look at them along a continuum, you'll see that the two are in fact intertwined.

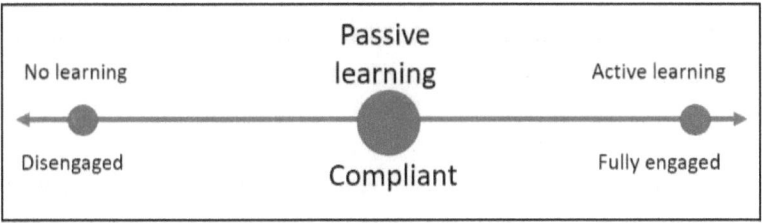

Figure 2: Learning & Engagement Continuum

On the left end of the continuum you'll see the worst-case scenario. Students are apathetic, misbehaving, or simply disinterested. Whatever the cause, disengaged students aren't learning much. In order to learn something, students must pay attention. These students, however, couldn't care less about whatever it is the teacher is droning on about. They want little to do with school and even less to do with learning.

The other end of the continuum embodies the ideal classroom environment. Students fully engage in the lesson. They are making meaning, asking questions, and diving deep. They are owning their learning and can't get enough of the content. These students are able to think flexibly about their knowledge because they are actively creating it. What they are learning is meaningful to them since it holds value and relevancy.

Compliant Classrooms

In the middle, however, is where most of our classrooms tend to default to. These students are listening to the teacher and filling in the worksheets. They are (mostly) paying attention while arranged in rows or silent table groups. They are sitting and getting. Passive learning, however, is nowhere near as powerful as active learning. In compliant classrooms, learning is being done *to* the students rather than *by* the students.

As a principal, compliant classrooms are deceptive. On the surface, they look adequate. There is a general order about the room and test scores generally pass muster. Learning done passively, however, remains the property of the teacher. Instead of incorporating new knowledge into their general memory, students instead work to cram as many facts as possible into short-term memory in order to spit them back out for the test.

The biggest problem with passive learning, however, is the type of thought processes they encourage. Passive learners tend to use more surface-level thinking strategies, such as rote memorization. As long as the tests match the teaching format, everything is great. Students start having problems, though, when they interact with new contexts. If they encounter a twist on existing knowledge or are asked to think creatively, difficulty ensues.

Engagement matters because degrees of learning exist. The more engaged students are, the greater the degree of learning. It's the fully engaged, active learners that are best able to succeed with complex, rigorous tasks.

Reference

Benware, C. A., & Deci, E. L. (1984). Quality of learning with an active versus passive motivational set. *American Educational Research Journal, 21*(4), 755-765.

Day 3

Question: Which type of learning (active or passive) do you cultivate in your classroom? What evidence do you have to support your claim?

_____
_____
_____
_____
_____
_____
_____
_____
_____
_____
_____

Action: Look back at a previous week's lesson plans and notice the difference in active learning and passive learning activities. Did you assign more worksheets/textbook questions or plan more engaging tasks?

Day 4: Motivational Theories

Student motivation impacts engagement and learning. If students don't buy into a lesson, the best that teachers can hope for is passive interest. Yet what was it that drives students in academic environments? Why do they sometimes become enthralled with an activity while at other times spurn learning as if it were the plague?

I knew that the answers to these questions could better inform teachers. I reasoned that if educators had a firm grasp on student motivation, if they could see the man behind the curtain, so to speak, they could use that information to their advantage. With knowledge of what makes students tick, instructors could design instruction that targeted student motivation. Instead of hoping and praying that the students would engage in learning, they could teach with confidence. Taking what they knew of student motivation, they can incorporate that into instructional design to better engage their young learners.

So I began to research student motivation. I figured it would be a simple task that could be completed shortly with a few well-constructed search terms. While I expected there to be a lot of information, I hoped it would be definitive. Surely there was agreement on what motivated students to learn, right?

I couldn't have been more wrong.

Motivational Theories

As I began my journey into the nether reaches of education psychology, I first ran across the expectancy-value theory of Wigfield and Eccles. Students' motivation, they found, depended on two major factors. First, students have a higher likelihood of engaging in learning if they expect to be successful. When a task seems doable, it encourages students to participate. Secondly, students need to find value in what they are learning. If it means something to them personally or it seems relevant to their interests, they'll be more apt to learn. Irrelevant tasks aren't worth the effort required to complete them and disengagement quickly follows.

Following up on the expectancy-value theory, I discovered the control-value theory put forth by Reinhard Pekrun. While the second elements of both, value, explored students perceived relevance of learning tasks, the first parts differed. For Pekrun, it wasn't enough to look at students' expectancy of success. Instead, he and his colleagues found that students' sense of control of their success played a pivotal part in motivation. Did students feel successful because the task was easy, something outside of their control? Or did they expect success because of their effort and ability, something within their control? More importantly, this theory sought to explain how control and value affected the emotions students felt during learning.

Feeling like I was homing in on the answer, I kept searching and found another major theory. The self-determination theory, researched by Deci and Ryan, added components I felt were missing to my growing understanding. This theory of human motivation puts forth three major areas that influence our actions: competence, autonomy, and relatedness. People are encouraged to participate, the researchers believed, if they feel competent for the task at hand. Additionally, having a choice (autonomy) plays a part since most people do not like to feel coerced. Finally, relatedness adds a personal element. If what they are doing relates them to others and builds relationships, it is highly motivating. This last part takes into account our social nature as humans, something that is oftentimes lacking in clinical theories.

Finding Commonalities

While I've just recapped the major motivational theories above, there are more that play into the final answer I found. If you'd like to peruse the entire review of literature, you may do so in Appendix 1. Instead of finding a simple answer, though, I found many. Some elements of the major theories explored in research worked well together while others seemed at odds. Sometimes I felt as if the researchers were using different words to describe the same things just so they could claim that their theory was original!

Looking at everything I found while researching, however, I began to notice commonalities. Some ideas cropped up again and again, not only as theoretical constructs, but also as experimental components. Students like to feel successful and those that don't expect to learn usually find what they are looking for. Some students will do anything for you if you present them with options but react like a cat being dunked in water if told what to do. My own experience validated what that major theories all put forth, namely, that if students don't value what they are learning, they're much less engaged.

One thing I learned as a professional educator, however, is that teachers can inspire students by cultivating relationships with them. That plays a part in motivation in addition to our feelings. Sometimes outside circumstances, like a nasty divorce battle or a dying grandparent, can derail learning long before students enter a classroom.

After a long and exhausting review of over thirty years of clinical research on student motivation, I found that five facets emerged. I placed these five into the acronym CRAVE (Competence, Relationships, Autonomy, Value, and Emotions). If educators can remember these five things, they can design engaging instruction that makes every student crave learning.

References

Deci, E. L., Vallerand, R. J., Pelletier, L. G., & Ryan, R. M. (1991). Motivation and education: The self-determination perspective. *Educational Psychologist, 26*(3-4), 325-346.

Niemiec, C. P., & Ryan, R. M. (2009). Autonomy, competence, and relatedness in the classroom Applying self-determination theory to educational practice. *Theory and Research in Education, 7*(2), 133-144.

Pekrun, R. (2006). The control-value theory of achievement emotions: Assumptions, corollaries, and implications for educational research and practice. *Educational Psychology Review, 18*(4), 315-341.

Pekrun, R., Elliot, A. J., & Maier, M. A. (2009). Achievement goals and achievement emotions: Testing a model of their joint relations with academic performance. *Journal of Educational Psychology, 101*(1), 115.

Pekrun, R., Goetz, T. T., & Perry, R. P. (2002). Academic emotions in students' self-regulated learning and achievement: A program of qualitative and quantitative research. *Educational Psychologist, 37*(2), 91-105.

Ryan, R. M., & Deci, E. L. (2000). Intrinsic and extrinsic motivations: Classic definitions and new directions. *Contemporary Educational Psychology, 25*(1), 54-67.

Wigfield, A., & Eccles, J. S. (1992). The development of achievement task values: A theoretical analysis. *Developmental Review, 12*(3), 265-310.

Wigfield, A., & Eccles, J. S. (2000). Expectancy–value theory of achievement motivation. *Contemporary Educational Psychology, 25*(1), 68-81

Day 4

Question: Which is more important for classroom educators - research or experience? Why?

_____
_____
_____
_____
_____
_____
_____
_____
_____
_____

Action: Think of your target student. Either ask him/her or imagine a conversation in which you discuss why s/he learns. What motivates him/her in the classroom?

Day 5: CRAVE Learning

Five facets of student motivation emerge from decades of educational research. These five areas, detailed below, are present in all students. Much like a personality profile, the descriptors below are used to inform rather than label learners. While reading about the five facets of motivation, you might recognize students, your children, or even yourself in the descriptions. While some facets are more dominant than others in students, the following areas are what motivate all students to learn.

Competence

Some students are highly motivated by competence. When they feel like they are able to accomplish a task, they feel engaged and ready to learn. They love building their proficiency through sequential learning. Most importantly, these students need to have an expectancy of success. If they feel like the task is too difficult and out of their reach, they will quickly lose interest.

I like to call these students Bowheads. When I envision predominantly competence-motivated students, I always picture a little girl on the first day of school. She's sitting in the front row with her Easter dress on, she has three pencils sharpened with a pad of paper ready, and she already has her hand up before the bell rings. She greatly enjoys worksheets, multiplication facts, and fill-in-the-blank quizzes. For the most part, the traditional education system is built for students like her. Follow the algorithm, memorize the facts, and success is sure to follow.

Relationships

Other students get much more out of the classroom when they have positive relationships with others. Usually the teacher, though sometimes with peers, these students need the connection of other human beings. They thrive on cooperative learning and working with a partner. They best process information by talking things out with a friend and they love to connect their learning to their own lives. Relational learners also thrive in the dramatic arts and literature, exploring the human condition and reveling in the stories of others.

I lovingly call these students Stalkers. In elementary school, they are the ones who bring their teacher a flower from recess. Every. Single. Day. In junior high, they will attempt to add their teachers as friends on Facebook on their thirteenth birthday. By the time they are in high school, they will know things about their teachers that they have no business knowing. They don't mean to be creepy, they just desperately crave a positive relationship with their teachers.

Autonomy

For some, the key question is not, "What are we learning?" but, "Do I have to?" A sense of control can make all the difference to some students. After being told what to do, what to learn, where to sit, and how to answer questions their whole life, some students need to break free. A lot of passive-aggressive behavior in the classroom is a result of teachers trying to exert too much control over these students. For every instructor that makes it her mission to keep order in the classroom, there are several students willing to accept that challenge head-on.

For these students, the term Captain comes to mind. These learners are the ones who like to organize games on the playground, enforce the rules of learning centers, and relish the opportunity to choose their tasks.

As long as they are the captain and everyone else acts as first mate, the world works just fine. When they feel coerced, manipulated, or just plain boxed in, they instinctively try to assert control over their learning and their lives.

Value

If you've ever been asked, "Will this be on the test?" or "How will this help me in the real world?", you're getting signals that you are instructing a predominantly value-motivated student. For these students, relevancy is everything. If what they are learning somehow connects to them, they learn easily. If it seems pointless or useless, however, engagement is elusive. Some students value learning for its own sake while others value learning to accomplish a goal. It might be earning good grades, helping accomplish a larger aim like getting into college, or landing a productive job. Either way, these learners evaluate learning tasks through the filter of value.

These students can be thought of as Real-Worlders. They, more than any other type of learner, need to see the relevance in what they are learning. For them, tasks that are not grounded in reality or that help them accomplish a goal are not worth doing. They despise busy work and can quickly check out if they think a teacher or substitute is simply going through the motions. On the other hand, when they work on a task valuable to them, they can quickly become engrossed.

Emotions

Finally, some students' emotions serve as their primary motivational facet. If the classroom is fun, or an activity is game-like, than they are all-in. If it's a more sterile, factory-like atmosphere, however, they will find it hard to muster enough energy to participate. A key emotion to cultivate in these learners is interest. When their curiosity is piqued, their natural inclination will be to explore and engage. If these students suffer emotional distress, either in or out of the classroom, it will greatly affect their academic behavior.

After seeing Pixar's *Inside Out*, it's hard to think of these students as anything but Rileys. In the movie, Riley is the main character. Personified emotions, such as Joy, Sadness, Anger, and Disgust, influence her actions and wreak all kinds of havoc. Like Riley, emotions-dominant learners can sometimes swing back and forth based on how they are feeling. They feed off of exciting environments but can quickly lose interest if they feel bored.

As previously stated, these facets of motivation should serve to inform educators rather than typecast students. Knowing what motivates students, teachers can leverage this knowledge to design instruction that engages all learners and increases active learning.

Day 5

Question: Which of these five facets motivates you the most as a learner? How does that impact your teaching style?

_____
_____
_____
_____
_____
_____
_____
_____
_____
_____
_____

Action: Use a CRAVE inventory (found in Appendix 2) to evaluate the motivational preferences of your target student or your class.

Day 6: The Power of Self-Beliefs

Emily, Rilee, and Jolee worked at their table on the multiplication assignment. Their class had just finished learning the standard algorithm for two-digit by one-digit multiplication with regrouping. After the teacher modeled a few problems for the class, she passed out a worksheet with 15 practice problems for each student to complete. Though they could ask their neighbors for help if needed, the students were supposed to complete the task alone.

Each girl had a different expectation for the task. Emily looked at the worksheet and sighed. She had learned her multiplication facts in first grade and learned how to do two-digit by two-digit multiplication last year in the second grade. Everything she did this year in third grade math seemed to be a repeat of what she had already learned. With little enthusiasm, she rushed through the assignment. She made several careless mistakes and spent most of her time talking to her friends and getting them off track.

Rilee, however, hated math. She knew she wasn't good in math because her dad told her so. She struggled with multi-step problems and still had to use her fingers to add math facts with large sums. Sometimes the teacher worked with her at a special table but oftentimes she was left to figure things out on her own. Numbers didn't make any sense to her so she spent her time scribbling or copying off Emily when she could.

Jolee looked forward to completing the worksheet. She knew most of her multiplication facts by heart and used a multiplication chart for the ones she forgot. The teacher's explanation made sense and she was ready to try the algorithm on her own. She felt like she was a good math student. Though she wasn't as smart as Emily, she usually figured things out if she kept at it long enough.

The Power of Self-Beliefs

The impact of how students view their own competence is quite staggering. Students who have high self-efficacy beliefs use more varied and conceptual learning strategies. They tend to operate at the higher end of Bloom's Taxonomy while students who doubt themselves use more surface-level strategies. Those who feel poorly about their abilities reinforce those expectations while preferring rote memorization and basic recall. High-competence students, however, are more apt to evaluate, synthesize, and summarize new information.

Students who feel competent also show more persistence when facing difficult tasks. Learning is rarely a linear endeavor. Instead, it usually moves forward in lurches, with one step backward for every two forward. Students with strong self-beliefs don't let the steps backward keep them down for too long. Those who doubt themselves, however, tend to view failures as validation of their incompetence and avoid taking intellectual risks.

Finally, students with positive self-beliefs have better overall academic performance. Henry Ford said, "Whether you think you can, or you think you can't - you're right." This sentiment sums up the power of self-beliefs. Students who think they are able to successfully complete tasks and perform well academically usually do so. Those, on the other hand, who think negatively about themselves usually find what they expect to find. Beliefs oftentimes dictate results.

Tiered Activities

One method teachers can use to build the competence beliefs of their students is to utilize tiered activities. The vignette of the three girls showed that giving every student in a classroom the exact same assignment can be very de-motivating. Of the three in the scenario, only Jolee found the task to be a good fit for her current ability level. Emily found the task too easy and her boredom distracted others. Rilee, conversely, found the worksheet beyond her perceived abilities. Instead of trying and risking failure, she found it easier on her self-esteem to not try at all.

Tiered activities works on the principal that every student is not identical. Though they might all be striving for the same goals based on the district or state curriculum, students are academically diverse. Using a Goldilocks-type approach, teachers can tweak tasks to operate at various levels so that students can find the best fit for their needs.

Tiered Examples

Assuming that Jolee worked on grade-level, traditional tasks will work well for her. Emily, who is more advanced in this particular topic, needs something a little more challenging. Sometimes that involves above grade-level work, (e.g. three-digit by two-digit multiplication) or an extension of the task at hand. Keep in mind that advanced students need work on their level, not a higher volume of grade-level work. For example, she could have been challenged to create three separate two-digit by one-digit multiplication problems whose product fell between 50 and 100 while using the digits 1-9 one time each.

While Emily needed a more rigorous activity, Jolee needed additional support. Instead of working on 15 problems, she would have been better served completing only five with the help of the teacher. Since she struggles with basic math facts, she should focus more on the conceptual aspects of multiplication rather than tackling an abstract algorithm. Concrete manipulatives should be used to help her first understand basic multiplication before working on grade-level content.

For those who would argue that tiered activities are not *fair*, I would counter that education is more about equity than it is equality. Equality treats every student the same, as the worksheet task in the opening vignette. That only works if every student is the same, and we know they are not. Equity, however, acknowledges the reality of an academically-diverse classroom and seeks to even the playing field. Equitable tasks, such as tiered activities, build competence and motivation in students.

References

Greene, B. A., Miller, R. B., Crowson, H. M., Duke, B. L., & Akey, K. L. (2004). Predicting high school students' cognitive engagement and achievement: Contributions of classroom perceptions and motivation. *Contemporary Educational Psychology, 29*(4), 462-482.

Liem, A. D., Lau, S., & Nie, Y. (2008). The role of self-efficacy, task value, and achievement goals in predicting learning strategies, task disengagement, peer relationship, and achievement outcome. *Contemporary Educational Psychology, 33*(4), 486-512.

Pintrich, P. R., & De Groot, E. V. (1990). Motivational and self-regulated learning components of classroom academic performance. *Journal of Educational Psychology, 82*(1), 33.

Wigfield, A., & Eccles, J. S. (2000). Expectancy–value theory of achievement motivation. *Contemporary Educational Psychology, 25*(1), 68-81.

Zimmerman, B. J. (1989). A social cognitive view of self-regulated academic learning. *Journal of Educational Psychology, 81*(3), 329-339.

Zimmerman, B. J. (2000). Self-efficacy: An essential motive to learn. *Contemporary Educational Psychology, 25*(1), 82-91.

Day 6

Question: Do you believe every student should be treated the same in your classroom? Why or why not?

_____
_____
_____
_____
_____
_____
_____
_____
_____
_____

Action: Take an assignment your students will complete within the next week. Using the task as the grade level model, design an upper and lower tier for students. If possible, collaborate with a teaching partner and assign the task together. Share the student reaction and work samples with your partner.

DAY 7: SELF-BELIEFS PREDICT SUCCESS

Researchers have long wondered how ability beliefs affect student academic performance. A series of longitudinal studies examined students from elementary school to high school and looked at several key issues. The researchers wanted to know if self-beliefs changed over the years and how they interacted with student achievement.

Two major findings emerged from the studies. First, younger children have more positive achievement-related beliefs than older children. Across the elementary years, children's ability-related beliefs declined. The largest drop, however, occurred when students transitioned from junior high to high school. The decrease in self-beliefs then continues on through graduation. As the ability beliefs dropped, so did the value students placed in those subjects.

Second, children's beliefs about their ability and their expectancies for success were the strongest predictors of grades in math. This predictive power is so shocking because it outperformed students' previous grades in the subject. When considering past academic performance and student beliefs about their abilities, the beliefs did a much better job of predicting how students actually performed.

Self-Beliefs Predict Success

The results of these studies should give educators pause. Somehow, some way, students become less confident in their abilities the longer they stay in school. Though optimistic and positive in early elementary school, years and years of education seems to erode student self-beliefs. This trend is frightening beyond the obvious reason of its negative impact on student self-esteem. Student self-beliefs tend to predict success better than past performance.

It was this finding that made me truly appreciate the power of students' self-concepts. When the researchers examined the students, their performance was better predicted by their beliefs than their previous grades. In other words, perceived ability is just as or more powerful than demonstrated ability. How, then, are teachers cultivating positive beliefs in their classroom?

One thought to keep in mind is that false confidence is not the same as positive self-beliefs. Teachers that layer compliments on their students, especially when they are undeserved, run the risk of achieving the opposite effect. Students can smell insincerity a mile away. If they believe that teachers are simply painting sunshine and daffodils without any basis, they'll lose respect for teachers and themselves. The surest way to boost student self-beliefs so that they feel smarter is to effectively teach them so that they actually become smarter.

Setting Goals

For students with minimal confidence, their past is cluttered with a trail of failed attempts at learning. For these students to feel successful, they must first take an academic risk and try to learn something new. If that isn't difficult enough, these students with large gaps in their learning need to successfully accomplish what they set out to do. If they could do this on their own, they wouldn't have the abysmal self-beliefs they currently hold.

Thankfully they have professional educators to guide them.

Oftentimes struggling students either don't know how to set goals or set unreasonable goals. The first thing teachers can do is to accurately assess these students' present levels of performance. Instead of starting with grade level expectations, begin with what they can currently do. Though their instructional levels will most likely be well below grade level, that's where they need to begin.

Work with the students to set reasonable, measurable, and timely goals. Teachers will most likely have to assist students with these criteria until they get used to setting quality goals. Reasonable goals are within the student's current ability range. Not too easy but not too hard, reasonable goals can be accomplished with some effort and cognitive stretching. Goals also need to be measurable. Simply saying, "I want to get better," doesn't allow the student to know when the goal has been met. Objective, quantifiable goals are much better than subjective, abstract goals. Finally, goals should be short-term rather than long-term. Even though passing the final course exam is measurable, it's too far in the future to be a useful tool if set in September.

Graphing Competence

One way to visualize student performance is to quantify it and have students graph their performance. For those with little success in learning endeavors, seeing a performance graph rise can completely change their self-image. This simple technique will empower students as they see a direct relationship between the graph and their performance. As they seek to improve the graph to see the line climb higher, they'll expend more energy toward their own learning. For the first time, they will feel like they can get smarter and will work harder and harder to make it happen.

Using the vignette from Day 6, Rilee demonstrated difficulty in basic addition facts. Before becoming comfortable with the idea of multiplication as repeated addition, let alone two-digit by one-digit multiplication, she needs to gain automaticity with her addition facts. A good goal for her might be to answer 20 questions correctly on a one-minute fact quiz. She can take a one-minute quiz each Friday until she meets her goal. When she gets 20 questions correct, she can either set a new goal of the same type (e.g., get 25 questions correct) or set a different type goal altogether (e.g, get 10 multiplication facts correct).

By utilizing regular intervals and quantifiable goals, she can record her scores each week on a graph. The graph can serve as a great tool to boost self-beliefs. Seeing her graph rise week after week will be solid proof that she's improving. If the graph's direction varies, it provides an opportunity for the teacher to conference with Rilee. They can discuss why the results aren't consistent and make a plan to improve. It's this type of reflective analysis that students with low self-beliefs need assistance with.

Reference

Wigfield, A., & Eccles, J. S. (2000). Expectancy–value theory of achievement motivation. *Contemporary Educational Psychology, 25*(1), 68-81.

Day 7

Question: What goals have you set for yourself as a teacher? Are they reasonable, measurable, and timely?

_____

_____

_____

_____

_____

_____

_____

_____

_____

_____

_____

Action: Find something within your discipline that occurs regularly (e.g., math fact quizzes, vocabulary tests, reading fluency assessments). Develop an opportunity for students to set goals and measure their performance on these tasks.

Day 8: Causes for Success or Failure

The four friends compared their tests as the teacher handed them back. Thankfully it was a practice test designed to prepare students for the final exam because none of the students passed the test. As they began to discuss their results, however, each student had quite a different spin on why they failed.

"I know why I failed," complained Danna. "The teacher has it out for us. He created a test with intentionally tricky questions. I'm not even sure he taught everything on the test. I think he wanted us to fail. The final exam is sure to be just like this one, so there's no hope at all."

"I'm not too sure about that," Jonathan replied. "Today just seemed like an unlucky day. My favorite sweater is in the wash, my sister ate the last Pop-Tart, and the teacher didn't have coffee this morning."

Danna retorted, "Coffee?!? What does that have to do with anything?"

"The teacher has coffee every morning except this morning. For some reason he didn't bring in his Starbucks and he's been grouchy the entire class period. I think as long as he has coffee on the day of the final exam, and I get my sweater washed, everything will be fine," Jonathan answered.

"You both are crazy," Danielle responded. "I know exactly why I failed - I'm stupid. I've never been good in school and neither was my mother. It doesn't matter if you spike the teacher's coffee with happy juice, nothing will change one simple fact. I won't pass this class."

"Well, that's depressing," Cliff said in reply. "For me, I know that I didn't try my hardest for this test. I didn't study last night, I haven't taken very good notes, and half of each class is spent listening to the three of you bicker. I'm going to ask the teacher to help me figure out the problems I got wrong. Between that and studying harder, I think I can pass the final exam."

Causes for Success or Failure

An influential theory of motivation is Bernard Weiner's attributional theory. With it, Weiner puts forth four main causes to which people attribute their success or failure. The first, represented by Danna in the vignette, is task difficulty. If students are successful, it's because the task was easy. If they fail, the problem again lies with the design of the assignment. Since task difficulty lies outside a student's control, failure attributed to this does nothing to motivate students to try again. If the task was too hard to begin with, the student has no ability to make it any easier in the future.

The second attribution is fate or luck. Represented by Jonathan, those that believe in a disembodied outside force subscribe to the power of random forces. If they succeed, there's no guarantee that they would get the same results if the scenario were repeated. If they fail, there's always a chance they could be luckier the next time. Still outside the control of the student, belief in luck is fickle and doesn't inspire extra motivation.

The third reason students give for success or failure is ability, embodied by Danielle. This is an internal attribution but still not under the control of the student. If they are successful and believe it is due to their intelligence, they will be encouraged to continue in the task.

However, if they fail and blame it on their ignorance, it will stop them in their tracks. Most students don't believe that they can get smarter overnight and a lack of ability can be very disengaging.

Finally, some students are like Cliff and attribute their results to their effort. Of the four attributions, this is the only one that research shows to motivate students in both success and failure. When students achieve due to their perceived effort, they see that success is within their control. They choose how hard they try in learning situations. If they fail, however, and attribute that to a lack of effort, they still remain in control of their destiny. They see that they should have tried harder and jump back on the proverbial horse to try again.

Exemplars and Rubrics

One way to help students build their competence and begin to believe in the efficacy of their effort is to frequently use exemplars and rubrics. For many students, hearing something once or watching a teacher demonstrate something a few times is not sufficient. They need additional support to successfully complete learning tasks. The use of exemplars and/or rubrics give students the necessary scaffolding to keep trying until they get it right.

Exemplars are simply completed examples or models that serve as a guidepost for students. Like practice problems at the beginning of a math lesson in a textbook, these illustrations show how to do something successfully. By patterning their work after the exemplar, many students can work through issues and discover solutions on their own. Oftentimes students can work backwards from a completed example and apply a similar process to their own problem. This serves to highlight how effort and persistence, not innate intelligence, help students achieve.

Rubrics, on the other hand, give structure to normally abstract tasks, such as writing. At times, subjective tasks seem hard to grasp for some students. Instead of being black and white, some learning activities require creativity, originality, and other hard-to-quantify elements. A well-written rubric, though, uses strong descriptors and action verbs to describe desired results. Students can use rubrics as a pathway to improvement, judging their work against higher and higher criteria. This also provides students with an opportunity to meet clear expectations for success and see the value of their effort.

Reference

Weiner, B. (1985). An attributional theory of achievement motivation and emotion. *Psychological Review, 92*(4), 548.

Day 8

Question: Think of your target student. When s/he fails, what does s/he think caused the failure? How does that impact motivation?

_____
_____
_____
_____
_____
_____
_____
_____
_____
_____
_____
_____

Action: Find something that you will teach soon that requires multiple steps. Create an exemplar that can be posted on the wall for students to reference as needed. If you are going to assign something subjective, like a large project or essay, include a detailed rubric so students can find a clear pathway to improvement.

Day 9: Growth Mindset

Lynne and Loretta loved dressing alike as often as possible. Growing up next door to each other, they were nearer to sisters than cousins. Their mothers were still close and set a wonderful example for their daughters. The girls were especially excited because they had the same fifth period science class at the junior high this year.

The cousins and their mothers all rode together for the first day of school. Driving up to the junior high, Lynne's mother gave her customary speech. "Remember, Lynne, that you are an intelligent girl. You always get straight *As* and your father and I expect nothing less. Remember that I graduated," Lynne's mother began.

"As the valedictorian of your high school," Lynne interrupted. "I know mom, you tell me every year."

"Don't you forget it," her mother answered. "You've always been smart and your grades should always reflect it."

Lynne rolled her eyes and Loretta snickered. Loretta's mother took the break as an opportunity to give her daughter a final thought before leaving the car. "Loretta, don't you forget that everything you've gotten is because you worked hard for it. Classes will be harder this year and you also signed up for a few pre-AP classes. You can get good grades if you work hard enough," Loretta's mother said.

"Thanks, mom," Loretta replied. "I know. I won't let you down."

As the girls exited the car, they talked about the rest of their classes. Though they shared a science class, they had no other classes in common. While Loretta elected to take advanced classes, Lynne stayed with basic classes and that kept the cousins apart most of the day. When Loretta asked Lynne why she didn't take any pre-AP classes, she responded quickly.

"Are you kidding me? Who wants all that extra work? And there's a chance that I might not make straight *As* with all that advanced material. I know that some consider a *B* in a pre-AP class the same as an *A* in a regular class, but that's just silly. I couldn't risk the chance of not making perfect grades."

Mindsets

The girls in the vignette embodied the two different mindsets researched by Carol Dweck. Lynne is a prototypical fixed mindset student. Those with a fixed mindset believe that intelligence or ability is fixed from birth. Some are born smart, some aren't. Some have athletic giftedness and others have difficulty walking and talking at the same time. Either way, abilities are relatively stable and students shouldn't try to reach above their intellectual station.

Loretta, on the other hand, exhibits more of a growth mindset. Students with a growth mindset believe that intelligence or ability is flexible. It can grow based on a person's effort and will. Quite literally, these students believe they can become smarter through determination and focus. Whether it be musical ability, academic ability, or even a physical skill, those with a growth mindset don't subscribe to the notion that one's abilities are static.

For learning situations, the two mindsets tend to encourage different attitudes in students. Fixed mindset students who have a favorable view of their intelligence, like Lynne, can become academically conservative and avoid risks. More than learning, preserving their view of their intelligence becomes of primary importance. For some, this means taking easier classes to ensure good grades. Fixed mindset students who believe they are unintelligent are in double trouble. Not only do they believe they are dumb, they don't think anything they do will change that.

It is the growth mindset students that are most comfortable with taking risks in learning new things. They welcome a challenge and see failure as informative rather than declarative. They believe that nothing is truly impossible.

Growth Mindset Feedback

In a recent article reflecting on growth mindset, Dweck commented that one way teachers can help students adopt a growth mindset is to legitimize the fixed mindset. Each girl in the vignette above served as a caricature of a certain mindset. In reality, people are mixture of both. Growth mindsets are not the light side of the Force while fixed mindsets embody the dark side. People have a little of both in them and that is nothing to be ashamed of. Attempting to ban a fixed mindset might lead to false growth mindsets.

The example with Loretta and Lynne utilized the praise of their mothers because, as educators, the praise we give students can oftentimes encourage a growth or fixed mindset. See the examples below from Carol Dweck of growth mindset encouragement and fixed mindset encouragement.

Growth Mindset Encouragement

- "When you learn how to do a new kind of problem, it grows your math brain!"
- "If you catch yourself saying, 'I'm not a math person,' just add the word 'yet' to the end of the sentence."
- "That feeling of math being hard is the feeling of your brain growing."
- "The point isn't to get it all right away. The point is to grow your

understanding step by step. What can you try next?"

Fixed Mindset Encouragement

- "Not everybody is good at math. Just do your best."
- "That's OK, maybe math is not one of your strengths."
- "Don't worry, you'll get it if you keep trying."
- "Great effort! You tried your best."

The final two fixed mindset responses might seem as if they are mislabeled. Actually, this type of encouragement embodies a false growth mindset. Trying fruitlessly won't help a child get smarter if poor strategies are being used. The point is to get the problem correct, not *try* to get it correct. Effort is important but doesn't replace performance. Praising less than optimal achievement as a good effort actually reinforces a fixed mindset. If students try their hardest and fail, yet receive praise, that communicates to them that they have done all they could and still missed the mark.

References

Blackwell, L. S., Trzesniewski, K. H., & Dweck, C. S. (2007). Implicit theories of intelligence predict achievement across an adolescent transition: A longitudinal study and an intervention. *Child Development, 78*(1), 246-263.

Dweck, C. (2006). *Mindset: The new psychology of success.* New York: Ballantine Books.

Dweck, C. (2015). Carol Dweck revisits the 'growth mindset'. *Education Week, 35*(5), 20-24.

Dweck, C. S. (1986). Motivational processes affecting learning. *American Psychologist, 41*(10), 1040.

Dweck, C. S., & Leggett, E. L. (1988). A social-cognitive approach to motivation and personality. *Psychological Review, 95*(2), 256.

Day 9

Question: Which type of praise do you most often find yourself giving students? How has that contributed to their mindsets?

_____
_____
_____
_____
_____
_____
_____
_____
_____
_____
_____
_____

Action: Use the suggested growth-mindset praise statements or find some additional ones on the internet. Make a series of index cards to keep on your desk so that you can refer to them throughout the day. Remember to praise the process, not the person.

Day 10: Influencing Competence Beliefs

Mr. McPherson finally had something to look forward to as an educator. Even though he'd been teaching at the high school for seven years, he was still the newest teacher in the mathematics department. This meant that he usually got stuck teaching the remedial courses. His days were filled with ninth and tenth graders attempting to make it past Algebra 1. Though he did the best he could, his results were less than stellar. His students came to him defeated and usually left in the same condition.

This year was going to be different, though. He looked at his roster for first period Algebra 1 and liked what he saw. The class was filled with freshman and each student name had a number beside it, ranging from 81 to 94. He couldn't believe it! 94! He had never taught a student who scored in the 94th percentile on last year's end of course exam. It looked like the school's move toward utilizing data for instruction finally resulted in him getting the pre-AP class he always wanted.

He looked at his lesson plans that he had been using year after year and knew they wouldn't suffice. These students performed in the top 20% on their math exam last year and they did not need remediation. No, what they needed was to be pushed. Instead of dawdling with basic properties of operations, he wanted to start the year out with a bold project-based learning task.

High Expectations

"Students, my name is Mr. McPherson. I'm so excited to be your teacher this year," he began on the first day of school. "I've been working with teachers in other disciplines and we've come up with something we think you'll enjoy." The students rolled their eyes but were definitely interested. "This project will start today and take the entire first month of school to complete. In connection with your science, English, and social studies classes, you will be working together to stop a serial killer.

"You and a group of three students will work as crime scene investigators to not only identify the murderer but also define the motive and how the killings take place. Clues will be scattered all throughout your classes and since I'm your first period teacher, I'll be serving as your base of operations. When you come across something you need help with, your job will be to go to the appropriate teacher and get the assistance you need. For instance, today we've received a coded message from the killer in the form of linear functions. If you can solve the equations, you'll crack his coded message and begin to unravel his devious plot," Mr. McPherson concluded.

A hand slowly shot up. "Uh, teacher, this all sounds hard. We've never done anything like this before. Are you sure you know what you're doing?" a student timidly asked.

"Of course I do, young lady. The school included your scores on last year's exams and I couldn't be happier. You are all very capable and I know you can do it. Let's get started!" Mr. McPherson replied.

Getting Started

The students looked at each other wordlessly and shuffled forward to receive the coded message. That first day didn't go over so well and Mr. McPherson had to do a lot of reteaching on linear functions. He figured they had just forgotten a lot over the summer and didn't let up on them. He constantly pushed them and challenged the class to extend their thinking because he knew that they had the ability to do great things.

At the end of the month, his students had solved the mystery of the serial killer. Working together as a group, with teachers in various classes, and even before and after school, the momentum slowly built until the class seemed like a juggernaut. They entered school each day ready to tackle the next task, confident in their ability to work through any problems and find success. Mr. McPherson was especially pleased with their performance and was planning the next set of lessons when he was called into the principal's office.

Percentile Scores

"Mr. McPherson," Ms. Miller began. "I understand that your first period class took a different approach to Algebra 1 this month. I was a little worried until I saw the results from our common assessment. Your students outperformed every other Algebra 1 class in the school, even the pre-AP courses. How did you do it?"

"Ms. Miller," Mr. McPherson replied, "Thank you very much. The students you gave me deserve all the credit. If they hadn't been so smart, none of this would have been possible. I am a little confused, though. You said my class outperformed the pre-AP courses. My first period is a pre-AP Algebra 1 class."

"No, it isn't. That's why your success is so amazing. What did..."

"I'm sorry to interrupt, Principal Miller, but I'm now very confused." Mr. McPherson brought out his roster. "Look at this roster. These students are mathematically gifted. See Heather here? She scored in the 94th percentile on her test last year."

As Ms. Miller examined the roster, she nodded and looked up. "I'm the one who needs to apologize. I guess I wasn't very clear on these numbers on the first period roster. You have the same type of students you always have, Mr. McPherson. Your first period class is a remedial Algebra 1 class, just like normal.

"These are their locker numbers off to the side."

Influencing Competence Beliefs

This story shows the silver lining in the dark cloud of student self-beliefs. While teachers cannot change how students perceive themselves when they enter their classroom, they have every opportunity to change those beliefs by the time they leave them. Research clearly shows that what a teacher believes is very powerful in influencing competence beliefs. More than anything, students will pick up on how their teacher views them and begin to mirror that in their own minds.

If teachers exhibit a growth mindset, they can begin to develop that in students simply by living it out. When they normalize errors, don't speak down to students who are struggling, and hold high expectations for all, students will begin to see themselves as capable. Sometimes the teacher's belief is all the fuel students need to begin to view themselves as competent.

Unfortunately, this truth works both ways. Negative teachers or those with a fixed mindset can instill those qualities in their students. People tend to find what they are looking for and students will often rise to the level of teacher expectations, both high and low.

References

Mueller, C. M., & Dweck, C. S. (1998). Praise for intelligence can undermine children's motivation and performance. *Journal of Personality and Social Psychology, 75*(1), 33.

Zimmerman, B. J. (2000). Self-efficacy: An essential motive to learn. *Contemporary Educational Psychology, 25*(1), 82-9.

Day 10

Question: What expectations do you have for your target student? Is s/he meeting those expectations?

_____
_____
_____
_____
_____
_____
_____
_____
_____
_____
_____

Action: Think about how your classroom is set up to support competence beliefs. Brainstorm with a teaching partner different ways you can better support your students' self-beliefs.

Day 11: Character by Osmosis

One of the best things about being a new teacher was the blissful ignorance I enjoyed. Being alternatively certified as an elementary educator, I honestly had no idea what I was doing those first few years. I taught on instinct rather than through pedagogical prowess. I couldn't tell you what was developmentally appropriate for my students more than I could describe a curriculum map. Somehow, some way, I muddled through long enough until I was able to get my feet under me.

Looking back on my beginning in education, there are a few things I accidentally got right. For the first two years of my teaching (2000 - 2002), I also attended classes at the local seminary. You see, I really had no interest in becoming a teacher. Education was something I was doing at the time to pay the bills. Fresh out of college and newly married, my overall plan was to enter the ministry, hence the seminary classes. Teaching was my day job while I toiled endlessly through my evening seminary classes and volunteered at my local church.

Though I didn't come right out and say that teaching was secondary, I shared with my students my hope of one day being a pastor. I brought my backpack to school and even showed them a few of my seminary textbooks. Not knowing any better, I opened myself up to them and talked with them about my goals. I let them know that I had homework just like they did. The fact that I went to classes at night after spending a long day with them seemed to impress them.

I had no idea how I was impacting their lives.

Character by Osmosis

Of all five facets of student motivation, relationships is probably the one best understood by teachers. They intuitively know that they can influence and motivate students simply by building relationships with them. Oftentimes, teachers enter the profession because of a teacher they had sometime during school. Many adults can point back to an educator that quite literally changed their lives forever.

Research has much to say on this issue. By modeling proper values, teachers can increase student persistence and goal-setting. This is one truth I inadvertently discovered as a novice teacher. My openness with my students and discussions about my schooling helped them with their own development. By exhibiting the traits I valued (e.g., persistence and goal-setting), I was actually instilling in them character by osmosis.

Students are deeply enthralled by their teachers. Seemingly insignificant hobbies, preferences, or activities can be awe-inspiring to students. With a captive audience for hours each day, teachers would do well to be intentional about their conversations. Take a few moments and consider what traits you'd like to see in your students and share personal stories highlighting those qualities. Teachers can do much to improve the character of their students by being purposeful about what they model.

Self-Regulation

Additionally, teachers often lament the lack of self-discipline students exhibit. It sometimes seems as if they have no filter for their thoughts but instead shout out anything that comes to mind. Studies also show that teachers can help students learn skills to regulate their emotions and behavior. They do this by building and nurturing positive relationships with students.

For many students, their teacher is the most emotionally stable person in their life. I can remember leaving parent conferences with sudden insights about why my students behaved the way they did. Working at an elementary school, I often served as the first male teacher my students had ever had. Within the community I taught, positive male role models were sometimes hard to find. For a few of my students, I was the father they never had.

Teachers teach much more than their content. They teach students how to think before they speak. They teach them to share and take turns. Teachers have the chance to help students learn to control their emotions by being a rock of surety in a chaotic world. This is done through building positive relationships that serve to motivate students to participate, engage, and achieve.

Class Meetings

Teachers should proactively build and nurture a positive classroom environment. Instead of hoping that amiable children get assigned to their care, teachers can utilize a technique called Class Meetings. These short groupings seek to set the tone for respectful learning and create a classroom climate of mutual trust. Class Meetings also honor individuals and increase their sense of significance. They create empathy, encourage collaboration, and support social-emotional learning.

Ideas for Class Meetings, sometimes called Morning Meetings, can be found by utilizing an internet search or combing through social media sites like Pinterest. Typically, these gatherings take place at the beginning of class and last anywhere from five to fifteen minutes, depending on time constraints. There are four main components of Class Meetings:

1. Greeting - Give the students the opportunity to practice greeting each other and the teacher. Sometimes, this basic skill is not a prevalent as teachers assume.

2. Sharing - Allow students a chance to relate important events and information in their lives. This builds a more open community

and helps them develop conversation skills.

3. Group Activity - This is the most structured part of the Class Meeting. Students participate in a brief, energetic activity, sometimes for building group cohesion, sometimes for practicing social or academic skills. Either way, it should be fun!

4. Announcements - Teachers close with a message to students. It might be motivational or a reiteration of a procedure. Sometimes teachers use this time to remind students of the focus for the day or to use a specific strategy.

References

Dabbs, L. (2013, September 18). *The Power of the Morning Meeting: 5 Steps Toward Changing Your Classroom and School Culture [blog post]*. Retrieved March 1, 2017, from Edutopia: https://www.edutopia.org/blog/morning-meeting-changing-classroom-culture-lisa-dabbs

Hamre, B. K., & Pianta, R. C. (2001). Early teacher-child relationships and the trajectory of children's school outcomes through eighth grade. *Child Development, 72*(2), 625-638.

Martin, A. J., & Dowson, M. (2009). Interpersonal relationships, motivation, engagement, and achievement: Yields for theory, current issues, and educational practice. *Review of Educational Research, 79*(1), 327-365.

Ryan, R. M., & Deci, E. L. (2000). Intrinsic and extrinsic motivations: Classic definitions and new directions. *Contemporary Educational Psychology, 25*(1), 54-67.

Day 11

Question: Which teacher had the biggest impact on you as a student? How did that teacher affect your life?

_____

_____

_____

_____

_____

_____

_____

_____

_____

_____

_____

_____

Action: Commit to trying a Class Meeting once or twice a week to build a more positive community. Start small and reflect often. If possible, ask your teaching partner to come observe a class meeting to provide feedback.

DAY 12: RELATIONSHIPS DEVELOP SELF-ESTEEM

Jasmine came to me as a troubled student. She had always struggled academically. Her reading was below grade-level expectations and English was not her first language. Mathematically-speaking, she had difficulty recalling basic facts and performing simple algorithms. She had all the classic signs of a student at-risk of failure.

All of that pales in comparison to her behavioral issues, however. She was irritable, stand-offish, and a drama queen. When she didn't have problems with the other girls in my classroom, she was devising ways to cause trouble. Her actions caused her to miss large portions of teaching, resulting in her falling further behind her peers. Her academic deficiencies sparked behavioral outbursts and a sensitivity to any kind of attention from me.

Despite all that, I liked her.

She had a spunk that was infectious. She was a fighter. What other teachers viewed as insubordination, I saw as spirit. She had been socially promoted year after year and arrived in my class desperately behind her classmates. The trouble, though, was that she knew it. If Jasmine had anything going for her it was social awareness. She had more street smarts than any student I had ever met. She intuitively understood social relationships and how to exploit them to get what she wanted. What she needed, I knew, was someone to believe in her.

I decided that students like Jasmine were why I was a teacher. I loved the challenge of teaching and sometimes got bored with only instructing able learners. Jasmine was going to learn, come hell or high water. Before I could teach her, though, I had to reach her. She viewed me with the same distrust with which she saw all her former teachers. To her, I was just the next in a long line of adults to give up on her.

Making Progress

More than anything, I remember Jasmine for the growth she made that year. Since I only had a few years of teaching under my belt, I didn't have an organized social-emotional program for my classroom. I didn't know much about character development or nurturing the soft skills of empathy, communication, and leadership. There was no magic elixir that I knew of to make Jasmine the subject of an after school TV special.

I decided to take a different approach with Jasmine. Rather than focusing on her deficits, which were numerous, I looked first at her strengths. She was snarky and sarcastic, two qualities I could appreciate in students. She was so into pop culture (e.g., TV and movie references) that she sometimes left her peers behind in conversations. So instead of ostracizing her because of her academic struggles, singling her out for additional remediation, we talked.

We talked about movies, her favorite TV shows, and anything else she found interesting. She responded well once she realized I wasn't tricking her into trying to learn something. Even though she rarely did any work, and the assignments she did turn in were either incomplete or incorrect, I focused first on building a relationship. I did it because I wanted to know her as a person, not in order to get something from her. I knew that she would smell insincerity a mile away and tried simply to be a positive adult role model for her.

Relationships Develop Self-Esteem

By the end of the year, Jasmine was unrecognizable. She had made some academic growth but was still below grade level. While the gains she made were nice, she still barely passed for the year. When I think of Jasmine, I don't think of how much I taught her. I'm not sure I actually did that much to advance her knowledge. The difference was in how she viewed herself.

She had (mostly) stopped getting in fights. She had many friends in the class and was viewed as a leader. School was no longer a prison for her but a place where she could become smarter. Her name was no longer feared in the teacher's lounge and her conduct marks virtually disappeared. She started to see herself as normal, something she had never done before.

What I knew instinctively at the time, but now understand through research, is that relationships can have a positive effect on the emotional states of students. Positive interactions with teachers and peers can energize the self and develop self-esteem. For students like Jasmine, they don't need to be fixed. They don't primarily need tutoring and academic remediation, though those are important. They first need a positive relationship with their teacher. Students are humans, not pieces of data.

Cooperative Learning

Building a positive teacher-student relationship is only the first piece of the motivation puzzle for some students. Being friends with the only adult in the room is all well and good, but if students still feel isolated from their peers, engagement will suffer. A frame of mind teachers can embrace to build student-student relationships is nurturing cooperative learning.

Cooperative learning is not group work. It is more than simply telling students to find a partner and complete a worksheet together. Instead, cooperative learning is a series of structures that organize social interactions. It purposefully encourages students to use each other as learning resources by defining roles and tasks during conversations.

One example is called Numbered Heads Together. This technique puts students in groups (e.g., four to a table) and then numbers each of them. When the teacher asks a question, student groups put their heads together to discuss the answer. Each member of the group should be confident in the answer because the teacher will then call one number randomly to share the group's answer.

Another strategy is called Three-Step Interview. Students pair up and take turns interviewing each other using teacher-created questions about the subject at hand. After each partner has asked and answered the questions, the third step has them report their findings to the entire class.

References

Hamre, B. K., & Pianta, R. C. (2001). Early teacher-child relationships and the trajectory of children's school outcomes through eighth grade. *Child Development, 72*(2), 625-638.

Kagan, S. (1989). The structural approach to cooperative learning. *Educational Leadership, 47*(4), 12-15.

Martin, A. J., & Dowson, M. (2009). Interpersonal relationships, motivation, engagement, and achievement: Yields for theory, current issues, and educational practice. *Review of Educational Research, 79*(1), 327-365.

Day 12

Question: Think of your target student. Are you more focused on academic deficiencies or him/her as a person? How does that impact the target student?

_____
_____
_____
_____
_____
_____
_____
_____
_____
_____
_____
_____

Action: Find a worksheet you have planned in the near future and replace it with a cooperative learning strategy. Instead of answering the questions on paper, encourage students to engage in meaningful conversations.

Day 13: Students Watch Teacher Interactions

James was a typical student. His grades were slightly above average and his work was usually turned in with only a few mistakes. He had a few friends in class and played well with others on the playground. Any notes sent home were returned promptly and he was as well-behaved as one could expect of a seven-year-old boy.

Unfortunately, he was in Mrs. Jackson's class. Mrs. Jackson had been teaching first grade since the first Bush administration. Two years away from retirement, Mrs. Jackson made it a point to keep her room neat and tidy. Her students all had assigned desks and cubbies. The students knew where to turn in their work, place their lunchboxes, and keep their school supplies.

Mrs. Jackson was a stickler for handwriting. By the time her students left her classroom for second grade, they could print neatly and some even knew how to write in cursive. She did not accept sloppy work but handed it back for the student to rewrite neatly. This is where James started having issues.

His fine motor skills were abysmal. He held a pencil like he was going to stab someone and he rushed through his work. It always looked as if he had written his spelling words with a dull pencil on top of a blanket. More often than not, Mrs. Jackson returned his assignments to him so that he could write them again neatly.

James obliged Mrs. Jackson the first few times because of his good nature. He wanted to please his teacher and diligently rewrote his work whenever asked. Unfortunately, the work he "fixed" oftentimes looked identical to the original. After a few tries, Mrs. Jackson simply gave James a failing grade and moved on. This pattern continued throughout the first month of school.

Changing Attitudes

By October, Mrs. Jackson's attitude toward James had changed. She began to see his lack of penmanship as an indicator of his ignorance. She started to speak down to him and treat him as an intellectual delinquent. Her comments to him were short and clipped. The less she saw or heard of him, the better. He was a stain on her teaching reputation.

The other students in the class noticed how Mrs. Jackson treated James. Subconsciously, they believed that her treatment of him was related to his academic struggles and poor behavior. James' classmates started to treat him in the same way. They viewed him as a troublemaker and a poor student. They disliked having to work with him as a partner and he started to play by himself on the playground.

All of this finally came home to roost in James himself. He saw how the teacher and his peers treated him. He began to internalize their actions and believe what they said about him. James started to think that maybe there was something wrong with him. Perhaps he was a nuisance and no good at school.

Students Watch Teacher Interactions

Multiple research studies by Jan Hughes and colleagues at Texas A&M University show that students watch teacher interactions with other students. Classmates witness how the teacher interacts with a child and begin to subconsciously assign the student an academic reputation, either positive or negative. By seeing what the teacher says to a student and what tone of voice is used, they relate that to how smart that student is.

Classmates take into account the character of teacher interactions with the student and integrate that into their view of the child's likability. If the teacher speaks positively with their classmate, they view that student as likable. Conversely, if the teacher seems angry at a student or overly uses sarcasm, the students notice that as well. Teacher-student interactions are absorbed by classmates into what the researchers call a peer academic reputation.

These factors then transmit to the student. Most students are aware of how they are viewed by their peers, picking up on small social cues and conversational tidbits. If their classmates see them as unintelligent, students can begin to incorporate those views into their own self-assessment. External beliefs become internal truths and students rise or fall to the level of social expectations. All of this can stem from how students watch teacher interactions.

Synthesis Squads

One method teachers can use to increase peer relationships in the classroom is a grouping technique called Synthesis Squads. As opposed to temporary groups that meet for a class period or two to complete an activity, Synthesis Squads can last for several weeks or months. Their purpose is to give students a sense of stability over time and deepen the relationship between students as they journey the school year together.

Teachers can design the squads to be composed of various learning preferences. One method would be to separate students by their modality of learning. For example, students can create triads of an auditory learner, a visual learner, and a kinesthetic learner. When new tasks are assigned, students can use their Synthesis Squad as a base of operations. Within the group, each student has one or more strengths to contribute toward learning.

Another way to organize students is by preferred learning style (i.e., mastery, understanding, interpersonal, and self-expressive). Mastery learners do best when remembering and summarizing. They enjoy clear sequences, expanding their competence, and measuring their success. Understanding learners, however, prefer using reason and logic. Mysteries that invoke their curiosity and opportunities to analyze and debate are highly motivational.

Interpersonal learners thrive while utilizing their social prowess. They learn best when relating the curriculum to themselves and others. Teams, cooperative learning, and even coaching motivate them through the energy they derive from relationships. Finally, self-expressive learners prefer to use their imagination and creativity. They are constantly asking "What if?" and trying new ideas out.

When learning something new, students working in Synthesis Squads have a better chance of understanding new material if the strengths in the group are varied. Where one type of learner might not understand how something is presented, another type of learner might quickly understand it.

References

Hughes, J. N., & Chen, Q. (2011). Reciprocal effects of student-teacher and student-peer relatedness: Effects on academic self-efficacy. *Journal of Applied Developmental Psychology, 32*(5), 278-287.

Hughes, J. N., & Zhang, D. (2007). Effects of the structure of classmates' perceptions of peers' academic abilities on children's perceived cognitive competence, peer acceptance, and engagement. *Contemporary Educational Psychology, 32*(3), 400-419.

Silver, H. F., Strong, R. W., & Perini, M. J. (2007). *The strategic teacher: Selecting the right research-based strategy for every lesson.* ASCD.

Tomlinson, C. A., & Imbeau, M. B. (2010). *Leading and managing a differentiated classroom.* ASCD.

Day 13

Question: Think of your target student. How are your interactions with that student interpreted by the rest of your class? How are you contributing to that student's peer academic reputation?

_____

_____

_____

_____

_____

_____

_____

_____

_____

_____

_____

Action: Use your observations or an inventory (a learning style inventory can be found in Appendix 3) to group your students into Synthesis Squads. Decide on a task for them to work on, either as a group or individually with the group's support. Reflect as a class on the usefulness of Synthesis Squads.

Day 14: Relationships Increase Achievement

Some elementary teachers love recess. It provides a nice break in the day and allows students a chance to get their wiggles out. Plenty of research shows the benefits of free play and recess has a positive impact on student attention and emotions. Yet when I began my education career as a fourth grade teacher in Fort Worth, TX, I dreaded recess.

The kids got to play and have fun for 15 or 20 minutes each day. All I had to look forward to was standing around with a bunch of really old teachers. They must have been in their 30s at least. Their favorite pastime was complaining about the principal, the parents, and their students. As a mature 22-year-old, I was not going degrade myself to that level. I was a professional educator, after all, and always attempted to carry myself with dignity and seriousness. I preferred gossiping with my wife in the privacy of my home.

There was a large open field in the back of the school that served as the main playing area. While the other teachers knotted together under a tree, keeping a wary eye on the playground, I volunteered to supervise the students playing soccer. I use the term *soccer* lightly, of course, because there was not a defined field to play on. Boundary lines were fluid and the only goals the students had were made by dropping jackets on the grass about twenty paces apart.

Regardless of the irregularity of the soccer field, the kids loved playing. Standing on the sideline (again, I use the term loosely), I would gaze longingly at the laughing children. I hoped that the ball would come my way every now and again so I could kick it back to the students. Then, one day, the temptation grew too great. As the students lined up on the field to perform the complex mechanism of balancing social status with athletic prowess (a.k.a. picking teams), I stood with them.

I wanted to play.

Accidental Motivation

Playing soccer with my students was the best thing I could have ever done. I had no idea at the time, but reflecting on that magical first year, I now see how large of an impact that had. Remember that my motivation for doing this was very selfish – standing around and adult-ing for 20 minutes every day was torture for a young first-year teacher. I didn't know that I was fulfilling the psychological need for relationships by playing soccer with my students. I was just bored, though my wife wasn't too thrilled after I ruined a second pair of pants with grass stains.

Because I played soccer with my students at recess, my students became putty in my hands in class. I was a young Anglo-Californian teaching in a predominantly Hispanic school in Texas. I didn't have the first clue about my students' worlds and, honestly, I didn't even know that I should even try to understand their background. Inadvertently, though, I had brought myself into their world by playing soccer. I had opened a connection with them and, for some, that was all they needed.

They might not have cared about the subjects I taught but they started to work hard for me. I developed a close relationship with them by letting them destroy me on a soccer field for 20 minutes a day. They saw me reach out to them and they reciprocated. The boys that I had the most trouble with because of their rambunctious nature in the classroom were the ringleaders on the soccer field. When I met them on their terms, they started meeting me on mine.

Relationships Increase Achievement

Positive relationships between students and teachers boost motivation and achievement. When students like their teachers, they are more willing to work for them. They feel connected and that link gives them purpose. Students who are close to their teachers, whose emotional needs are being met, are more motivated to learn.

This increase in motivation translates into learning and achievement. Students are more apt to engage in instruction and reach the level of active learning when they relate positively to their teacher. More learning leads to increased achievement. Sometimes, the key to raising test scores has more to do with personal relationships than it does with teaching techniques.

For students highly motivated by relationships, the teacher-student relationship is foundational. If that isn't in place, the rest of what the teacher wants to do doesn't really matter. We need to enter their worlds and relate to them personally before worrying about textbooks and homework assignments.

Fingerprint Your Lessons

Every teacher can't play soccer at recess. Secondary teachers don't even have that as an option. While it worked for me my first two years of teaching, it didn't translate to the next school I taught at. The point is not to play but to become a real person. For most teachers, this will come through their lessons. Instead of reading off a script, teachers need to make their instruction feel personal. The more personality that becomes visible in their teaching, the greater the relational rewards.

Students find their teachers very interesting. Sometimes abnormally so. Rather than hide themselves away from students, teachers should exploit that attention. Tell stories about your children, bring pictures of your vacation, and share your hobbies with students. If you're reading a good book (that's appropriate), bring it to school and talk about it. The more of you the students can see, the better.

One of the worst pieces of advice I've ever heard for new teachers is, "Don't smile before Christmas." The (lack of) logic behind this gem is that to keep discipline in the classroom, teachers should be stern and forbidding. Yet learning, not management, is the first priority of teachers and students. For students highly motivated by relationships, a friendly teacher is essential. I've seen many classrooms that were well-ordered but lacked active learning. One does not necessarily precede the other.

References

Christophel, D. M. (1990). The relationships among teacher immediacy behaviors, student motivation, and learning. *Communication Education, 39*(4), 323-340.

Martin, A. J., & Dowson, M. (2009). Interpersonal relationships, motivation, engagement, and achievement: Yields for theory, current issues, and educational practice. *Review of Educational Research, 79*(1), 327-365.

Roorda, D. L., Koomen, H. M., & Spilt, J. L. (2011). The influence of affective teacher-student relationships on students' school engagement and achievement: A meta-analytical approach. *Review of Educational Research, 81*(4), 493-529.

Ryan, R. M., & Deci, E. L. (2000). Intrinsic and extrinsic motivations: Classic definitions and new directions. *Contemporary Educational Psychology, 25*(1), 54-67.

Wentzel, K. R., & Wigfield, A. (1998). Academic and social motivational influences on students' academic performance. *Educational Psychology Review, 10*(2), 155-175.

Zimmer-Gembeck, M. J., Chipuer, H. M., Hanisch, M., Creed, P. A., & McGregor, L. (2006). Relationships at school and stage-environment fit as resources for adolescent engagement and achievement. *Journal of Adolescence, 29*(6), 911-933.

Day 14

Question: Have you brought yourself into the classroom? How are you leveraging natural student interest for increased motivation and achievement?

_____

_____

_____

_____

_____

_____

_____

_____

_____

_____

Action: Bring a hobby to school to share with your students. It doesn't have to serve an academic purpose. Instead, the point is to make yourself more relationally accessible to your students.

Day 15: Relationships Help At-Risk Students

Jasmine (from Day 12) made a lasting impact on me. At the end of that year, I had been a teacher for four years, all of them in the fourth grade. Growing a little restless, I decided to move up to fifth grade the following year. I did it not only to take on a new challenge but also to continue my work with Jasmine. I didn't want everything she had accomplished to disappear the following year if she got matched up with the wrong teacher.

There was a problem, however. By moving up, I lost my seniority on my grade level and became the newest fifth grade teacher. For some unknown reason, not enough fourth graders returned the following year. As the year began, each fifth grade class had about 17 students. Meanwhile, on the other side of town, a different school had too many sixth graders (about 28 in each class). Since I was certified up through sixth grade, you can probably guess what happened next.

The week after Labor Day I was involuntarily transferred to teach a self-contained sixth grade class. Yep, that's a thing. I had 22 sixth graders all to myself. Every. Single. Day.

I was not ready for that school. Those children, I hate to admit, ate me for lunch. I had to make sure my professional attire displayed only gang-neutral colors. In a district with over 50 elementary schools, there was only one alternative elementary school for students with discipline problems. Assistant principals fought tooth and nail to get one student from their entire campus placed in that school. I had five from my class placed there that year.

I felt like I was the winner of some kind of inverted educational lottery. Did I mention that most of my students had perfect attendance that year?

Hardest Year Ever

That was the hardest year of teaching I ever faced. Honestly, I only made it through with lots of prayer and reassessing everything I thought I knew about teaching. My students didn't want to learn. They saw no future in education and normally only came to school because their parents kicked them out each morning. They had given up on themselves.

It took me a while, unfortunately, to remember the lessons I had learned from Jasmine the previous year. I was so appalled by the misbehavior in the classroom that I instinctively took a controlling approach. That was the worst thing I could have done. I might as well have tossed gasoline on a fire for all the good my attempts at classroom management were. When it came to subverting authority, these students were true professionals.

After a near breakdown because of my utter failure in teaching my students, I changed my approach. I stopped worrying about every little thing they did to disrupt instruction and tried to roll with things a bit more. I made a giant game board on a bulletin board and at the end of each day we'd play for a few minutes. It was based on Chutes and Ladders and, no, they never knew. The giant slide connecting box 87 and 24 owned them.

Slowly but surely, most students came around. There were a few I never reached but I stopped taking it personally. I went to work each day, tried my best to relate to the students, and let the chips fall where they may. As soon as I started focusing on my students as people rather than a collection of educational deficiencies, I began to build relationships with them. That, more than anything else, was what they needed.

Relationships Help At-Risk Students

As stated on Day 14, positive teacher-student relationships boost motivation and achievement. For students who are at-risk of failure, though, academic success is significantly more likely when influenced by a positive teacher relationship. Whether it be teen pregnancy, domestic violence, serious health issues, or a host of other contributing factors, at-risk students need relationships before they'll be interested in learning.

Education is built on the assumption that students are emotionally stable and eager to learn. Teachers base their instruction on the belief that students are interested in making themselves smarter. For most students, this isn't an issue. When children come to school from a steady home environment and no glaring survival needs (e.g., food, shelter), learning can proceed as planned.

However, some students have much larger concerns than passing a high-stakes test. If they don't know where their next meal is coming from or where they'll sleep that night, learning is unimportant. If their parents are going through a nasty divorce or if they are dealing with substance abuse, everything else is secondary. For teachers to teach, they must first reach through the mess and connect to their students.

Response Chaining

Building relationships between students is just as important as nurturing healthy teacher-student relationships. Too often, class discussions or partner talk involves students speaking past each other rather than with each other. A technique that teachers can use to encourage productive student talk is called response chaining.

When asking questions of the class, teachers can disengage their students by following the traditional ask-and-answer routine. A teacher asks a question, calls on one student to answer, and 24 other students lose interest because they aren't involved in the conversation. Instead, teachers can put students into groups of six to eight and show them how to chain their responses together.

Teachers first ask a question of students. One member of the group answers the question while the others listen. The next person in the group responds but chains his/her response to the first answer. It can be an agreement, disagreement, or extension of the original answer, but it must somehow connect. The next person then chains his/her response to the first and/or second student's answer, and so on.

Reference

Roorda, D. L., Koomen, H. M., & Spilt, J. L. (2011). The influence of affective teacher-student relationships on students' school engagement and achievement: A meta-analytical approach. *Review of Educational Research, 81*(4), 493-529.

Day 15

Question: Of your students that are at-risk of failure, what is your primary focus? Building a relationship or filling in their academic gaps?

_____
_____
_____
_____
_____
_____
_____
_____
_____
_____

Action: Take your next set of chapter review questions and have students use response chaining with them. Make sure to model it first with a sample question. After response chaining, students can select a few questions and answer them for the assignment.

Day 16: Keys for Intrinsic Motivation

If you are a parent, you've most likely had an eye-opening experience when your child was very young. Something happened during the toddler years that gave you an insight into the character of your child. For better or worse, you briefly glimpsed your next 15 or so years raising this wonderful little human being.

For example, I remember when I learned that my daughter was a dinosaur.

At the time of this writing, Desiree is a beautiful eleven-year-old on the cusp of middle school. Yet when she was just two-years-old, something happened that gave my wife and me a peek into her motivational needs. Heather, my wife, was going grocery shopping with Desiree at a local grocery store. As often happens, Desiree got hungry while shopping and wanted a snack.

Her food of choice was a cereal bar and Heather was adequately prepared. Desiree snacked on her bar while Heather slowly meandered up and down the aisles of the grocery store, replenishing our stock of necessities (e.g., cereal bars). The problem occurred when Desiree finished her snack. She was fine holding the wrapper while eating the cereal bar because she didn't completely unwrap the bar. Instead, she treated the wrapper like a banana and only peeled enough away to expose the next portion of bar.

Once the bar was finished, though, she was left holding the empty wrapper. The horror! For some reason, her dignity as a toddler was deeply maligned by touching a piece of trash. Naturally, she tried giving Heather the wrapper to hold. However, my wife was busy pushing a cart, crossing items off a grocery list, and placing food in the basket. Her hands were full and she did not think of herself as a walking trash can.

She told Desiree to hold the wrapper. And then normal existence crumbled.

A T-Rex is Born

By my daughter's reaction, my wife was afraid an innocent bystander would feel the need to call child protective services. If we had told Desiree to hike barefoot across the Sahara desert with a single juice box, I don't think she would have been as upset. The indignity of having to hold her own trash was a spectacle to behold, full of raw emotion and desperation. After holding the wrapper against her will for the duration of the store, Heather checked out at the register and they left. On the way out, she saw a trash can and pushed the cart over to it.

"Desiree," Heather started, "thank you for holding the wrapper. We're all done now and you can throw it away in the trash can." Even though Desiree had been screaming like a banshee for the last 15 minutes, Heather was trying to put a nice spin on it. Desiree, though, wasn't having any of it.

"It's too far," Desiree claimed. The basket was six inches away from the trash can. Heather pushed the cart against the trash can, removing the offending chasm. Now easily in reach for a toddler, Heather again asked Desiree to throw the wrapper away.

"It's too far," Desiree repeated again, a defiant smirk on her face.

"No, honey, it's not. Just stretch out your hand," Heather said with an exasperated sigh.

"I can't," Desiree said definitively. With that she became a T-Rex, a dinosaur with disproportionately small arms. Desiree attempted to move her unaccountably deformed appendages but to no avail. Somehow, within the last 15 minutes, both of her arms had shrunk and she no longer had the ability to move them more than a few inches. Strange how that happens at the worst possible times. Needless to say, it took an extra five minutes at the trash can for Desiree gain enough dexterity to throw the wrapper away.

Keys for Intrinsic Motivation

What my daughter was exerting throughout that episode was her need for control. Known as autonomy in the field of educational research, many students are driven by their need to control as much of their life as possible. Whether it be within the classroom or at home, the power of choice is a strong factor in learning situations.

Many teachers wish that their students would be more intrinsically, or internally, motivated to learn. Tired of coaxing, prodding, and sometimes bribing students to participate, it would be much simpler if students acted of their own accord. If they learned because they wanted to rather than because they had to, persistence and achievement would rise.

Yet research shows that there are two keys for intrinsic motivation. The first is competence, described in detail in Days 6 through 10. For students to even have a chance of motivating themselves, they must first feel they are able to accomplish the task at hand. The second key is autonomy. Students who feel forced to do something might be motivated but that driving force is extrinsic, or external. When the outside factor goes away, so does the motivation. If teachers want their students to motivate themselves to learn, they need to cultivate an atmosphere of competence and autonomy.

Portfolios

When looking to increase students' sense of autonomy, even the most basic pieces of instruction should be scrutinized. One aspect of education that most take for gospel truth is homework assignments. Teachers assign them, students do them, and the cycle repeats endlessly. However, there is a great opportunity to increase motivation if teachers weave some portfolios into the mix.

Portfolios can support student autonomy if students are active participants in their creation. When teachers mandate a certain number of artifacts to be included and dictate how each one should be crafted, all student control lies is lost. Rather, students should have choice over which pieces to include in the portfolio and perhaps even how many items to submit. Students use higher level thinking as they analyze their work, searching for the best pieces to include to meet established criteria.

Two main types of portfolios are growth portfolios and assessment portfolios. As the name suggests, growth portfolios should demonstrate a student's growth over time. Some possible items for students to include are early and late pieces of work within a unit, pretests or other quizzes, or even rough drafts and final drafts. Additionally, students can include growth reflections, progress reflections, or goal-setting sheets.

Assessment portfolios, on the other hand, are more focused on specific curriculum standards. Instead of simply using a final test to evaluate knowledge gained during a unit, assessment portfolios allow students to prove to the teacher that sufficient progress has been made toward mastery. Possible artifacts for submission are tasks aligned to learning standards, projects or real-world applications, or performance tasks. In addition, cumulative tests, rubrics, or reflections on content mastery could be included.

References

Niemiec, C. P., & Ryan, R. M. (2009). Autonomy, competence, and relatedness in the classroom Applying self-determination theory to educational practice. *Theory and Research in Education, 7*(2), 133-144.

Ryan, R. M., & Deci, E. L. (2000). Intrinsic and extrinsic motivations: Classic definitions and new directions. *Contemporary Educational Psychology, 25*(1), 54-67.

Shernoff, D. J., Csikszentmihalyi, M., Shneider, B., & Shernoff, E. S. (2003). Student engagement in high school classrooms from the perspective of flow theory. *School Psychology Quarterly, 18*(2), 158.

Day 16

Question: How have you seen the need for autonomy manifest in your target student? How much does the need for control play into his/her motivation?

_____
_____
_____
_____
_____
_____
_____
_____
_____
_____
_____

Action: Examine an upcoming unit and choose a type of portfolio (growth or assessment) to include. Decide how many items to require for the final product and how the assignments you already have planned fit into that. Make sure to give students some flexibility on what to include in order to support intrinsic motivation.

Day 17: Persistence and Regulation

It's hard to consider autonomy without thinking of my daughter Desiree. While Day 16's story gave a sneak peek into her motivational needs, lots of children act defiant as toddlers. That's just a part of being a two-year-old. Last year, however, when she was entering fourth grade, my wife Heather took her back-to-school shopping at Old Navy. It was there that Heather made one of the biggest mistakes in her entire tenure as a parent.

She said an outfit looked cute.

They had just walked into the store and several mannequins were on display with clothes for sale. As expected, some of the more enticing combinations were up front. Heather saw a shirt that said *Love Your Selfie* and matching jeggings. Being a good mother, she knew Desiree's style and figured that combination would be appealing to her. Yet she spoke without thinking and suggested the outfit for our daughter.

Will some people never understand parenting?

Quick Recovery

Heather immediately knew she had made a mistake. Desiree gave her a withering stare and stomped off to the other side of the store. Heather had committed the ultimate *faux pas*. Desiree was angry, embarrassed, and frustrated with my wife's seemingly controlling nature. What was she going to do next, remind Desiree to wash her hair?

Desiree spent over ten minutes "looking" at clothes on the other side of the store. She roamed aimlessly, moving hangers around and not really getting anywhere. The problem was, Heather was right about the outfit up front. It was Desiree's style and she wanted it. She couldn't, however, let Heather know it. That would be admitting that her mother was right - completely out of the question.

Thankfully my wife recovered quickly from her blunder and moved away from the offending outfit. She gave our daughter some space and kept an eye on her from across the store. Like a shark slowly circling its prey, Desiree's "looking" brought her ever closer to the *Love Your Selfie* outfit. Heather kept a respectable distance, picked up a few other items, and moved to the checkout line. Desiree saw her and joined her with the shirt and jeggings in tow. Without a word between them, Desiree placed the items alongside the few things Heather had picked up and they checked out together. In the end, Desiree chose what to buy.

It's still one of her favorite outfits.

Persistence and Regulation

As discussed on Day 16, intrinsic motivation requires both competence and autonomy. Students who are internally motivated to learn exhibit greater persistence in learning environments. By nature, learning involves taking academic leaps. There will inevitably be times when students come up against something they don't understand. It is in those moments of cognitive struggle that students construct knowledge. Yet if they give up too easily, if they quit before they push through the obstacle, learning will suffer.

This is where motivation becomes essential. Students who are participating because of internal motivation are much more resilient in these situations. If teachers want their classes to stick with something until they get it, they would do well to develop their sense of autonomy.

When students feel like they have some choices, like they are in control (to a degree), their intrinsic motivation and persistence will increase.

Additionally, intrinsic motivation helps students regulate their emotions. If you have students who seem to constantly melt down or have rapid mood swings, they might not feel in control. Like caged beasts, sometimes children lash out in an attempt to order their lives. Heather's reaction to Desiree's anger at Old Navy demonstrated this principle perfectly. If Heather had scolded Desiree, told her to stop acting like a baby, or even demanded that she get back over to where my wife was, Old Navy would now be referred to as ground zero. Instead, Heather gave her space. She let her "look" for clothes all on her own without trying to influence her. In the end, Desiree calmed herself and begrudgingly picked the outfit my wife suggested. Enough time elapsed, however, so that it was Desiree's choice.

May-Do/Must-Do

Teachers can do much to support student autonomy by how they structure recurring assignments. Most classrooms have something that happens on a weekly or even daily basis, such as vocabulary tests, review tasks, or working with math facts. The typical arrangement is for teachers to assign every task to every student. Some do it with relish, eager to please, while others work slower than molasses on a frozen Christmas morning. Rather than fighting this reality, teachers can classify their tasks into two categories: may-do and must-do.

Must-do tasks are simply traditional assignments. It is into this category that most repeating tasks will fall. Students must complete their spelling work, review sheets, or daily reading logs. This doesn't change anything regarding normal work, just what it is called. It also sets up a nice contrast with may-do tasks.

Most lessons have some nice extension activities included, either by the textbook or by teacher ingenuity. Yet oftentimes not every student is ready for these tasks. They are either bogged down by the regular assignment or aren't motivated to do anything extra. Teachers can classify these tasks as may-do. Just like they sound, students can choose to do these tasks or choose not to. The key lies in giving them the choice.

Picking Desiree up from school one day, she jumped in the car and talked non-stop about this new thing her fourth grade teacher had introduced called may-do/must-do. As I heard the excitement in her voice, I immediately saw the motivational power of this arrangement. Whereas before she mainly completed work to remain in compliance with the teacher's wishes, she now eagerly finished all her must-do work as soon as possible so she could choose a may-do task to complete. It was the choice that mattered.

References

Cordova, D. I., & Lepper, M. R. (1996). Intrinsic motivation and the process of learning: Beneficial effects of contextualization, personalization, and choice. *Journal of Educational Psychology, 88*(4), 715.

Pintrich, P. R., & De Groot, E. V. (1990). Motivational and self-regulated learning components of classroom academic performance. *Journal of Educational Psychology, 82*(1), 33.

Day 17

Question: Think about your target student or one of your own children. How does the need for autonomy affect his/her emotional regulation? What normally happens when you try to exert more authority?

_____
_____
_____
_____
_____
_____
_____
_____
_____
_____
_____
_____
_____

Action: Implement may-do/must-do on a small scale in the next week or two. Take the tasks you have already decided upon and label them as must-do. Then bring out an extension activity for students to work on if they finish their may-do tasks. Note how many take you up on your offer.

Day 18: Autonomy Fuels Creativity

We all go through phases in our life. Every so often, an idea will inspire us and we'll work diligently to pursue it. Whether you call it creativity or innovation, part of what makes us human is the ability to see beyond the here and now. Our minds are capable of visualizing vast designs from just a flicker of imagination.

In my early adulthood I went through a singer-songwriter phase. I knew enough chords to play basic songs on my guitar. I could carry a tune (with the help of a bucket), though my voice would never be called beautiful. My childhood was strongly influenced by the parody song style of "Weird" Al Yankovic. Put all that together with life in a college dorm and strange things began to happen.

If I figured out the chords to a popular song, I would start trying to come up with some alternate lyrics. My alma mater, California Baptist University, was graced with several of my creations. My personal favorite is *Sweet Home Cal Baptist*, a knock-off of Lynyrd Skynyrd's *Sweet Home Alabama*. I also was inspired by my living arrangements to change Bob Seger's *Old Time Rock N Roll* into *Old Time Dorm Room Smell*. Yes, I was going through a classic rock phase as well.

Pattern Blocks

Though the creative spark flared for just a few years, it wasn't the first time I'd been inspired. I can remember being enthralled by pattern blocks in the first grade. I couldn't tell you the name of my teacher or even the school I attended in first grade but I remember the creations I made. My teacher allowed students to play with the pattern blocks at the back table when they finished their work. That permission was all I needed and my goal everyday was to complete my tasks efficiently to build massive patterns using the blocks.

I remember the awe of seeing how the yellow hexagons fit with the green triangles. I always started small and then built a repeating pattern that spiraled out from the center. Every day was an opportunity to see how I could rearrange the blocks into new and unique designs. I'm sure I learned more in first grade than the fact that two red trapezoids or three blue rhombuses equaled a yellow hexagon. I just can't remember any of it.

Autonomy Fuels Creativity

Most of you could share similar stories of creative inspiration. A common theme that would most likely emerge is autonomy. When students have the ability to choose their tasks, many good things happen. First and foremost, autonomy fuels creativity. Intrinsic motivation, dependent upon competence and autonomy, greatly improves our imagination. For creativity to truly ripen, it must be nurtured in an atmosphere of freedom.

Too often, when students feel controlled, creativity is the furthest thing from their minds. Instead, a good portion of their mental capacity is consumed by thoughts of their situation. Whether planning ways to re-exert dominance or sullenly fuming about their predicament, students placed within tight boundaries are not apt to innovate.

Autonomy inspires more than creativity, however. It also leads to deeper conceptual learning. If you'll remember from Day 3, there are degrees to learning. One of the main purposes of this book is to help teachers move students closer and closer to active learning. Full engagement flows from many things, one of which is autonomy. Students think more conceptually when it's their choice to learn.

Additionally, autonomy surprisingly also increases recall of information. When students participate in learning of their own volition, the thinking strategies they employ are often more complex. This leads to greater achievement and increases the impact of what they learn. If teachers want students to not forget what they learned once the test has been turned in, increasing autonomy is a great place to start.

Reporting Formats

Too often teachers get stuck in a rut of how students show their knowledge. A seemingly endless supply of worksheets can sometimes keep teachers from getting creative with how students demonstrate their understanding. Ease supersedes individuality and every student hurtles toward the same product. One worksheet cannot possibly meet the needs of all the students in a classroom, let alone an entire grade level. Thankfully, teachers can demand student demonstration of knowledge while remaining flexible on how they accomplish that.

Many different options exist for allowing students the ability to choose the format for reporting their knowledge. While every student might be learning the same thing, how they each indicate that learning can be varied. To be honest, which teacher doesn't dread project reporting day? Do we honestly need 25 dioramas of the Alamo? Allow students a choice in how they prove their knowledge and watch creativity blossom.

Each reporting format should have its own rubric and a completed exemplar or two so they can see what a quality work sample looks like. Written, oral, or recorded reports, dramatic presentations, or debates are just a few formats students can choose. They might provide a demonstration, create a graphic novel or comic strip, or even type a blog post. The imagination of students serves as the only limit to the possibilities for showing their understanding.

Students (and teachers) should not view reporting formats as being easier than a traditional worksheet or project. By giving students a choice, teachers are giving up some control while also asking for higher quality. Instead of a free-for-all, students would need to ensure that their chosen task meets all the requirements set forth by the teacher. When students have a say in what they do, their creativity and conceptual thinking will be greatly enhanced.

References

Benware, C. A., & Deci, E. L. (1984). Quality of learning with an active versus passive motivational set. *American Educational Research Journal, 21*(4), 755-765.

Deci, E. L., Vallerand, R. J., Pelletier, L. G., & Ryan, R. M. (1991). Motivation and education: The self-determination perspective. *Educational Psychologist, 26*(3-4), 325-346.

Dickinson, L. (1995). Autonomy and motivation a literature review. *System, 23*(2), 165-174.

Ryan, R. M., & Deci, E. L. (2000). Intrinsic and extrinsic motivations: Classic definitions and new directions. *Contemporary Educational Psychology, 25*(1), 54-67.

Day 18

Question: How have you been inspired in the past? Did your creativity come from your own desires or because you were told to do something?

_____

_____

_____

_____

_____

_____

_____

_____

_____

_____

Action: Think about an upcoming assignment and replace it with student choice. If your students are not familiar with various reporting formats, start small and let them choose between a few options. Each choice should have a rubric or exemplar for students to reference. You can also keep an "Other" choice available for students to use if they think of something outside-the-box to pursue (with your permission).

Day 19: Structure Supports Autonomy

Mr. Doe knew that something wasn't working in his classroom. No matter how hard he tried, he never seemed to get through the entire lesson before the bell rang. He felt as if he was running a race through quicksand - every step forward made him fall farther behind. He racked his brain trying to get to the bottom of his teaching dilemma. If he couldn't figure it out, he knew some of his students would fail for the year.

He followed the curriculum map of the district perfectly. Instead of trying new things on his own, he stuck with the research-based lessons put together by the local instructional experts. He knew that his content knowledge was up to par. In fact, sometimes he felt like he knew too much about science. Although he understood what students needed to learn, he had a hard time transferring that knowledge to them.

Not wanting to wallow uselessly, he asked a colleague to come and observe him during an off period. "I need fresh eyes on the problem. If you could, please come and sit in the back of the room. Take in the whole atmosphere and tell me where I'm going wrong," Mr. Doe said.

Mrs. Sanchez, his colleague, agreed and watched his 4th period class the following Monday. Mr. Doe tried to keep everything as normal as possible so his teaching partner would get a representative sample of his teaching. Once again, he started out with high expectations for the lesson. Mr. Doe knew what he needed to do and how the students would demonstrate their understanding. However, the bell rang all too early and the students left with a part of the lesson still unfinished.

Feedback

When Mr. Doe met up with his colleague, he was nervous and excited at the same time. While he didn't like the idea of being deficient in some way, he desperately wanted to improve.

"So, what's the verdict? How horrible am I?" he started in joking tone.

Mrs. Sanchez quickly reassured him, "Nothing that bad. Your teaching technique was good. You obviously know what you are talking about. The students respect you and want to please you."

"Then what? I know I'm missing something," Mr. Doe replied.

"Let's talk about sharpening pencils," Mrs. Sanchez answered. "What's the procedure your students follow for sharpening their pencils?"

"I'm not sure what you mean," Mr. Doe said. "They just sharpen their pencils."

Mrs. Sanchez answered, "Not exactly. Two students sharpened their pencils during the first few minutes of class with no incident. But Nancy tried to do the same thing a few minutes later and you became annoyed with her. What was the difference?"

Clarity

"Well, Nancy should have made sure she had more than one sharpened pencil before I started instruction. I don't like me students to get up while I'm teaching," Mr. Doe explained.

"Sure, lots of teachers have that rule. When did you share this expectation with your students?" Mrs. Sanchez pressed.

"I guess I never did. So, what, my classroom would magically improve if I clarified my pencil-sharpening strategies?"

"Perhaps. There were a few other things I noticed. When class started, some students worked on a task they picked up from the back table. Others sat and talked until you moved to the front several minutes after class began. At that time, you berated the students who were talking because they should have been working on the back-table task. Yet that expectation wasn't posted anywhere for students to see. I think I've figured out your main problem. Your students don't know what you want from them. You lose a lot of time redirecting students to meet unspoken expectations," Mrs. Sanchez concluded.

"I always thought my students understood what they needed to do. How can I become clearer?"

Mrs. Sanchez replied, "Think about everything you want from students and pretend it's the first day of school. Spell out exactly what you want them to know and do. If possible, model procedures so that they can see it and hear it at the same time. If you set clearer expectations for what they should do at the beginning, middle, and end of class, you'll probably find enough time to finish your lessons."

Structure Supports Autonomy

While it may seem counter-intuitive, providing structure actually supports autonomy and motivates students. If students are left guessing as to what they should do, it can set them on edge. Instead of being free to pursue learning tasks, they are left wondering whether they are doing the right thing or not. When unclear or missing expectations lead to teacher outbursts, students confidence in their ability to function properly begins to drop.

Students need enough information and support to operate self-sufficiently in the classroom. They should be clear on behavioral and academic expectations. Additionally, they need to know how much latitude they have within the rules. Do they need to follow instructions step-by-step or do they have some leeway as long as they get the job done? When possible, choose the latter. Providing expectations is not the same as micromanaging. When students know what they must do and have some choice in how they accomplish the task, motivation skyrockets.

Clear Expectations

Decisions abound in the classroom. Some are extremely important, some are inconsequential. To support autonomy, students should have choice when possible. Yet the need for order in the classroom demands that some expectations are laid out by the teacher. Use the questions in the table on the next page to explore how you can clarify what you want students to do. As you answer them, ask yourself whether or not your students could confidently state your expectations.

Table 1: Structure Questions

Beginning Class	During Class	Ending Class
How is homework turned in? Does it need to be in a certain bin by a certain time of the day/period?	Where are the directions for the current activity displayed?	When should students get packed up the end of class?
Is there a starting task (e.g., bell ringer)? If so, how long do they have to complete it? Will it even need to be completed? Turned in?	Can they use the restroom or get a drink of water during class? If so, what's the procedure for getting permission?	Does anything need to be picked up before students leave?
What will signal the beginning of class (e.g., teacher's voice, a bell, a signal, announcements)?	How will the teacher get the students' attention? How should the students respond to this signal?	Does classwork need to be turned in before students leave or can they finish it at home?
Where can students find missing work if they were absent the previous day?	What should students do if they don't have supplies (e.g., pencil, paper, folder, binder)?	Can students stay after class for a few minutes to finish something up?
Should students be in their seats before the bell rings?	When can students use the pencil sharpener?	Is classwork turned into a different tray than homework?
Where should students place their backpacks?	How will students get recognized to talk?	How will students be signaled to dismiss?

References

Benware, C. A., & Deci, E. L. (1984). Quality of learning with an active versus passive motivational set. *American Educational Research Journal, 21*(4), 755-765.

Cordova, D. I., & Lepper, M. R. (1996). Intrinsic motivation and the process of learning: Beneficial effects of contextualization, personalization, and choice. *Journal of Educational Psychology, 88*(4), 715.

Deci, E. L., Vallerand, R. J., Pelletier, L. G., & Ryan, R. M. (1991). Motivation and education: The self-determination perspective. *Educational Psychologist, 26*(3-4), 325-346.

Dickinson, L. (1995). Autonomy and motivation a literature review. *System, 23*(2), 165-174.

Koestner, R., Ryan, R. M., & Bernieri, F. H. (1984). Setting limits on children's behavior: The differential effects of controlling vs. informational styles on intrinsic motivation and creativity. *Journal of Personality, 52*(3), 233-248.

Ryan, R. M., & Deci, E. L. (2000). Intrinsic and extrinsic motivations: Classic definitions and new directions. *Contemporary Educational Psychology, 25*(1), 54-67.

Zimmer-Gembeck, M. J., Chipuer, H. M., Hanisch, M., Creed, P. A., & McGregor, L. (2006). Relationships at school and stage-environment fit as resources for adolescent engagement and achievement. *Journal of Adolescence, 29*(6), 911-933.

Day 19

Question: What are some unspoken expectations you have for your students? How have you communicated and/or modeled them for your classes?

_____
_____
_____
_____
_____
_____
_____
_____
_____
_____
_____
_____
_____

Action: Look at the questions on the previous page and consider if your students could answer them as readily as you. Take a few answer to these questions and set forth clear expectations for your students in these areas.

Day 20: Control Kills Autonomy

Lunch duty.

I'll just let that sit there for a moment while you recover.

If you are an educator that has been blessed with this wonderful opportunity, I can name several things you'd prefer. You'd rather have a root canal without any pain-numbing medication. Binge-watching The Wiggles for 12 straight hours with your bratty niece would have more upside. Some of you might even elect to discuss politics with your in-laws before being sentenced to lunch duty.

I had the pleasure of being condemned to lunch duty for two years. I was a new principal of a charter school and we were just a tad understaffed. On a campus of 525 elementary students, there was no assistant principal, instructional coach, or full-time counselor. There was me and only me. Thus, for about two hours each day, I was doomed to try and keep over 150 students "under control" for 30 minutes at a time. If Dante were an administrator, he would have added an extra circle of Hell called lunch duty.

As always, my students educated me much more than I taught them. They showed me, for instance, that silent lunch is indeed a punishment. The only problem is, it punishes the adult rather than the students. First and foremost, you can't make students be silent. They either choose to talk or choose to remain quiet. This idea of forcing kids to do something is laughable.

Group Dynamics

The biggest lesson I learned from my students dealt with the intricacies of group dynamics. The children I worked with were, for the most part, polite and amiable. They got along well together and respected their teachers. Yet when congregated in large groups, such as in the cafeteria, a mob-like mentality overtook them. Their behavior could change from respectful to riotous in a matter of moments.

This was never more evident than when I tried to institute five minutes of silence on the entire cafeteria because of too much noise the previous day. I would make my pronouncement with my authoritative, principal voice. While normally the students and I respected each other's roles, for some reason they took silent lunch as a challenge. I sometimes believed they had misheard me and thought I had asked them to try and whisper as much as possible without getting caught.

I roamed the aisles in between tables, straining my ears and watching mouths. Was that student covering his mouth to talk or to cough? Was that a sneeze or a laugh? The more control I tried to exert, the less control I actually had. When the odds are 150 to 1, that's usually a losing bet. I'm not proud of the fact that it took me several failed attempts at using silent lunch before I realized that it didn't work. The only one being punished was me.

I turned normally well-behaved children into miscreants by a misguided need for order. While it makes logical sense that restricting talk due to an excess of talk would be a natural consequence, it simply doesn't work. The more educators try to dictate student behavior and actions, the more students will fight against them. It isn't malicious, just human nature.

Control Kills Autonomy

Though the example above refers to a non-instructional setting, the detrimental effects of control extend to the classroom. Teachers who exert too much control over their students or the environment counteract student motivation. For some students, the restrictive nature of certain teachers focuses their attention on what they can't do rather than what they can. Those strongly motivated by autonomy will see rigidity as a challenge to overcome.

Additionally, many teachers use tangible rewards as a form of motivation. Some teachers give extra credit, some primary teachers have a prize box. While this works for some students, it can have the opposite of its intended effect for autonomy-driven students. They will see the rewards as coercion and resent the perceived attempt at manipulation.

Finally, teachers sometimes put pressure on students to perform well, either in class or on important assessments. While it might come from good intentions, students can chafe at the compulsion. Some students have been known to purposefully fail a high-stakes test to spite their teacher or school. The more control teachers attempt to exert, the more it slips from their fingers. Like trying to tighten your grasp on a fistful of sand, adding more pressure is not a viable solution.

Top Three/Bottom Three

At the beginning of each school year, teachers go through the annual ritual of creating a class set of rules. Sometimes it works well to build a consensus of shared beliefs and expectations. Sometimes it's just easier to buy a pre-made poster of rules at a teacher supply store and slap it up on the wall. For those wanting to support autonomy and improve behavior at the same time, try the steps below to make a top three/bottom three set of class rules.

1. Have students work independently to create their top three positive behaviors and bottom three negative behaviors to avoid. Once each student has a personal list to operate from, put them

in small groups of four to create a composite list.

2. Each group should take their six behaviors (top three/bottom three) and create a representation for each. A visual symbol, like the international symbol for "No U-Turn", will help identify behaviors quickly through visual stimulation.

3. Have each group present their top three/bottom three to the class. They should share their visual representations and a rationale for each rule.

4. Create a class set of rules. The teacher should guide a class discussion looking for commonalities among group presentations. Allow students an opportunity to group similar proposals together.

5. Commit to the class rules. Once the class has decided upon the top three/bottom three, post them along with their visual representations in a prominent place in the classroom.

6. Once a week, discuss one of the top three/bottom three as a class. Allow students to comment on how that rule is working and what needs to be done to improve its use in the classroom. A great method for doing this would be utilizing Class Meetings as described on Day 11.

References

Deci, E. L., Vallerand, R. J., Pelletier, L. G., & Ryan, R. M. (1991). Motivation and education: The self-determination perspective. *Educational Psychologist, 26*(3-4), 325-346.

Erwin, J. C. (2004). *The classroom of choice: Giving students what they need and getting what you want.* ASCD.

Koestner, R., Ryan, R. M., & Bernieri, F. H. (1984). Setting limits on children's behavior: The differential effects of controlling vs. informational styles on intrinsic motivation and creativity.

Journal of Personality, 52(3), 233-248.

Niemiec, C. P., & Ryan, R. M. (2009). Autonomy, competence, and relatedness in the classroom Applying self-determination theory to educational practice. *Theory and Research in Education, 7*(2), 133-144.

Ryan, R. M., & Deci, E. L. (2000). Intrinsic and extrinsic motivations: Classic definitions and new directions. *Contemporary Educational Psychology, 25*(1), 54-67.

Ryan, R. M., & Grolnick, W. S. (1986). Origins and pawns in the classroom: Self-report and projective assessments of individual differences in children's perceptions. *Journal of Personality and Social Psychology, 50*(3), 550.

Skinner, E. A., & Belmont, M. J. (1993). Motivation in the classroom: Reciprocal effects of teacher behavior and student engagement across the school year. *Journal of Educational Psychology, 85*(4), 571.

Day 20

Question: What are some areas in which you try to exert too much control? How effective are your attempts?

_____
_____
_____
_____
_____
_____
_____
_____
_____
_____
_____

Action: Look at your class rules and consider if they are still relevant. Even if it's the middle of the school year, it's not too late to use top three/bottom three to improve motivation and engagement.

Day 21: Value Matters

School is important to students. Until it isn't.

If you think about it, our entire education system is built on one enormous assumption. Everything educators do in the classroom revolves around this single truth: if we assign it, students will do it. How often do you as a teacher question whether or not your students will comply with your wishes? Unless you work at a challenging school, this concern might not have ever crossed your mind.

In my education career I never worried about compliance. I taught, they listened and did the work. For the most part, that cycle never became interrupted while I was in the classroom. In addition, most teachers have children of their own. Like growing up in church if your father is the pastor, teachers' kids face an additional set of expectations. Their behavior reflects not only on them but also on their parents as teachers. Usually, having educators' children in your classroom is welcome because they know twice over what they're expected to do.

Yet that message never quite sunk in for my son Dave. Since he's my oldest, he has the honor of being the first child to experience new things in our home. While I wouldn't exactly call him the parental guinea pig, he might say it's a fitting description. He was the subject of our first parent-teacher conference. He was the first to participate (and quit) in school sports and band. He was also the first to fail a semester of a high school course.

Checked Out

The problem began when he checked out of chemistry. He still showed up every day but listening and working on assignments were two separate matters. He felt his teacher didn't want to be there. His analysis of her teaching style made me cringe as a professional educator because it was so on point. The teacher seemed bitter, apathetic, and simply assigned textbook chapters to the students to work on while she completed assignments for her master's degree.

This is where I learned the value of value. He didn't care too much for chemistry but that in itself isn't shocking. Most high schoolers find it hard to generate interest for certain subjects. Yet what most teachers (and parents) bank on is the value they place in achieving something. Whether it be getting a good grade, graduating as valedictorian, being admitted into a certain college, or even earning a high school diploma, most students can muster up the motivation to push through seemingly meaningless classes.

But what happens if they don't?

Dave had none of those goals. There was nothing inherent in passing the class that he found motivating. The teacher did nothing to try and engage him or his classmates. My disapproval also held no sway over him. Only by stripping away all the assumptions did my wife and I work out a compromise with him so that he would work just enough to eke out a passing grade. When students find instruction meaningless, motivation and engagement suffer greatly.

Value Matters

Students who perceive that a task has value for them are more engaged in the task. As an elementary educator, I rarely ran into disinterested students. Developmentally, most of my students were still in the pleasing stage, working on assignments to fulfill my expectations. It was my brief foray as a sixth grade teacher (Day 15) that first gave me a glimpse of how important value is to motivation. Students will only work because the teacher wants them to for so long. Eventually, the worth of a task must become internal.

For some students, it's enough if the task or class helps them attain a goal. While they might not care about the subject, it can be a means to a desirable end, such as earning a grade or counting toward a scholarship. Many students will comply with teacher wishes for an ulterior motive. Ideally, students will cherish learning for its own sake. Unfortunately, that's not always the case. If they find the instruction as helpful toward accomplishing a goal, that will usually be enough.

Also, some students find educational value in what they are learning. They see how what the content will help them become smarter and thus engage with instruction. Some teachers are adept at highlighting the general utility of their subject. If students see that what they are learning will help them in life in general, that can serve as motivational fuel. Somehow, someway, students typically need to find value in what they are learning.

Designing Tasks

Students are much more likely to find value in tasks if teachers spend a few moments thinking about their design. Fill-in-the-blank worksheets and copying definitions out of a dictionary are fluff work and students know it. When planning instruction, tasks that are assigned merely to fulfill a need to generate a numerical grade for a gradebook are hardly meaningful. Will the task help them learn something new? Will it activate prior knowledge or help them make connections? How does it fit into the larger picture of the curriculum unit? Will the students have gained something valuable by completing the task?

In addition to providing meaningful tasks, teachers should also provide diversity and novelty in what students do in class. Even the most interesting task can become dull if repeated time and time again. This is one of the major problems with religiously following a textbook as a curriculum guide. As thorough as the included tasks might be, they tend to be highly repetitive. Teacher-made (or teacher-found) tasks interjected into the curriculum guide can add some different flavors to the tasks teachers assign.

Reasonable challenges can be the difference between boredom and frustration. Each child operates at a slightly different ability level so what may be an easy task for one child might be arduous for another. Tiered assignments (Day 6) provide challenge because students can choose the just-right task for their instructional level. By designing tasks that can be achieved with teacher guidance, learning something new becomes a realized goal in the classroom and helps guide students to finding value in challenging tasks.

References

Ames, C. (1992). Classrooms: Goals, structures, and student motivation. *Journal of Educational Psychology, 84*(3), 261.

Cole, J. S., Bergin, D. A., & Whittaker, T. A. (2008). Predicting student achievement for low stakes tests with effort and task value. *Contemporary Educational Psychology, 33*(4), 609-624.

Greene, B. A., Miller, R. B., Crowson, H. M., Duke, B. L., & Akey, K. L. (2004). Predicting high school students' cognitive engagement and achievement: Contributions of classroom perceptions and motivation. *Contemporary Educational Psychology, 29*(4), 462-482.

Pintrich, P. R., & De Groot, E. V. (1990). Motivational and self-regulated learning components of classroom academic performance. *Journal of Educational Psychology, 82*(1), 33.

Weiner, B. (1985). An attributional theory of achievement motivation and emotion. *Psychological Review, 92*(4), 548.

Wentzel, K. R., & Wigfield, A. (1998). Academic and social motivational influences on students' academic performance. *Educational Psychology Review, 10*(2), 155-175.

Day 21

Question: Think of your target student. Do you think s/he finds your instruction valuable? Does s/he participate out of compliance or because the class helps him/her learn something new?

_____

_____

_____

_____

_____

_____

_____

_____

_____

_____

Action: Think about a task you've recently assigned to your students. Evaluate it through the lenses of meaningfulness, diversity, and challenge. How high do you think students would rank the task in each of those three areas? How could you have tweaked the assignment to increase its value?

Day 22: Mastery Goal Orientation

I never intended to write a book. I just wanted to understand what went wrong with Jenny.

During my time as a principal, I instituted stricter rules about missing work for students. Those that chose not to turn anything in eventually made their way to my office. I spoke with them, disciplined them, and tried to set them straight. Like the claims on a can of Lysol, it worked for 99.9% of my students. Jenny was the one that got away.

I tried everything with her. I ranged from hard-nose disciplinarian to friendly counselor. No matter what I tried, she had no interest in doing her work. Punishments, threats, parent conferences - all useless. She beat out the clock, made it to May, and somehow managed to be promoted to the next grade. She didn't come back the following year and I've never seen her since.

In all my years of education, both as a teacher and as an administrator, I've never been so stumped. I could understand outright defiance, anger issues, or even mental health concerns. Jenny, on the other hand, was politely non-compliant. The more frustrated I got, the calmer she became. I never reached her. I never found a way to motivate her to learn.

Years after my experience with Jenny, I still couldn't completely move on. Something nagged at me, making me think that I was missing something. I felt like I was looking at education with blinders on. While I could see what was in front of me, there were things in the periphery that I couldn't quite make out. From an adult perspective, everything should have worked for Jenny. The instruction, systems, and support were all there. Jenny simply had no interest in learning.

Driven to Research

I began to think more and more about student motivation. What was it that drove students to learn? Why did some students fully engage while others disengaged? While all of this was bouncing around in my mind, the issue with Dave (Day 21) was ripening. I realized that I needed to figure out what motivated students to learn, not only for professional reasons, but for my own children as well.

I looked through a few books and realized that most of the existing literature marketed toward teachers focused mainly on engagement strategies. Student motivation, not a bag of tricks to make my classroom fun, is what I was looking for. It didn't take long to realize that I couldn't find what I needed by getting a book from Amazon. I'd have to figure it out myself.

With a prolific use of Google Scholar, I began searching with basic phrases like *student engagement* and *student motivation*. The volume of what popped up was staggering, to say the least. I decided to focus on theories and research found in peer-reviewed publications, such as *Educational Psychology* and *Journal of Personality and Social Psychology*. I went to the experts to see what they had to say.

What I found has been briefly recapped on Day 4. What began as a simple internet search led me deeper and deeper down the rabbit hole. I'd find something that made sense and look for corroborating articles to support it. As I did that, more and more facets of student motivation emerged. When I finally finished researching, I realized that I had something worth sharing. Though I never would have done all that work if it was an assignment or a task, I pushed myself to the furthest limits because I wanted to learn. I needed to figure out student motivation.

Mastery Goal Orientation

I didn't realize it at the time, but while researching student motivation, I was exhibiting what research calls a mastery goal orientation. This frame of mind supports thinking patterns that sustain student involvement. I, as the student, spent months and months of my limited free time reading articles with titles like the ones listed in the references below. I'd stay up late at night and get up early on the weekends to keep reading. What sane person would do that?

In this endeavor, I valued learning itself. I wasn't trying to write a book, though that eventually happened. The only goal I had was to better understand students. Though I had Jenny and Dave at the forefront of my mind, I knew that whatever I learned would benefit all the students I worked with. That's what kept me going when my eyes were swimming at midnight. I was exhibiting the motivational facet of value because what I was doing mattered to me. It provided all the fuel I needed.

When students have a mastery goal orientation, they value learning for its own sake. Instead of working toward a goal or complying with teacher wishes, they learn because they want to. This motivation helps them pursue beneficial learning tasks. When they face obstacles or come across something that stumps them, they are driven to push past it. Whereas students working to earn a grade might give up when things get fuzzy, those who are participating to learn (rather than to achieve) have an additional drive. They fight through because what they are learning has real value.

20 Time

For many years, Google had a policy known as 20 Time that encouraged its employees to spend 20% of their time working on personal projects that they felt would benefit the company. This initiative, which has since disappeared, brought Google many new innovations, including Google News, Gmail, and Adsense. Educators have taken this idea and transferred it to the classroom, sometimes calling it Genius Hour.

Whether called 20 Time or Genius Hour, the idea behind this initiative is quite breathtaking. Rather than being told what to do, students can work on something that is meaningful to them. However it's structured, this philosophy greatly increases student motivation by generating a mastery goal orientation in learners. By letting them work on projects they find valuable, innovation and endurance will increase.

I would suggest teachers slowly work into 20 Time. Start with modified versions for limited amounts of time. Many students have never had to direct their own learning and complete freedom could be paralyzing. Rather, encourage them to research something that is related to a classroom topic, such as renewable energy or geometric designs. Provide time limits and checkpoints for students so they can receive feedback on their progress. Once they become used to learning for their own sake, some of the restrictions can be lessened.

References

Ames, C. (1992). Classrooms: Goals, structures, and student motivation. *Journal of Educational Psychology, 84*(3), 261.

Ames, C., & Archer, J. (1988). Achievement goals in the classroom: Students' learning strategies and motivational processes. *Journal of Educational Psychology, 80*(3), 260.

Barron, K. E., & Harackiewicz, J. M. (2001). Achievement goals and optimal motivation: testing multiple goal models. *Journal of Personality and Social Psychology, 80*(5), 706.

Grant, H., & Dweck, C. S. (2003). Clarifying achievement goals and their impact. *Journal of Personality and Social Psychology, 85*(3), 541.

Liem, A. D., Lau, S., & Nie, Y. (2008). The role of self-efficacy, task value, and achievement goals in predicting learning strategies, task disengagement, peer relationship, and achievement outcome. *Contemporary Educational Psychology, 33*(4), 486-512.

Linnenbrink, E. A. (2005). The Dilemma of Performance-Approach Goals: The Use of Multiple Goal Contexts to Promote Students' Motivation and Learning. *Journal of Educational Psychology, 97*(2), 197.

Schunk, D. H. (1990). Goal setting and self-efficacy during self-regulated learning. *Educational Psychologist, 25*(1), 71-86.

Day 22

Question: When have you experienced a mastery goal orientation? What motivated you to push through obstacles when learning something new?

_____
_____
_____
_____
_____
_____
_____
_____
_____
_____

Action: Work with a teaching partner to implement a modified 20 Time. Find an upcoming unit of study and build in some time for students to research related topics of their choice. If they've never done anything like this before, set a short time limit (one to two weeks) and provide time in class for students to work on their research. It should result in a simple product or presentation.

Day 23: Teachers Influence Goal Orientations

Mr. Jennings and Ms. Sharper had been teaching colleagues for five years now. Their rooms were next door to each other and they helped each other out if an emergency arose. They also began planning together a year ago and their lessons improved. They enjoyed bouncing ideas off each other and creating synergistic ideas. The attitude of their students, though, showed a marked difference.

While they generally stayed together in their pacing and materials, for some reason Ms. Sharper's class seemed to have a different feel to it. Her students seemed more enthusiastic about learning. They eagerly awaited each day's tasks, jumping into them with relish. While his class did the same assignments and heard the same lessons, their attitude was totally different.

"Will this be on the test?" was one of the most frequent questions he heard in his class. Right up there was the common query, "Is this for a grade?" For whatever reason, his students were overly interested in the exact role their tasks played in their class grade. If he didn't assign some numerical value to the task, he noticed that his students barely generated enough interest to finish.

He asked Ms. Sharper if he could sit in on her class during 7th period. He'd already taught the lesson they'd planned together multiple times that day and he wanted to see what she did differently. He tried to be inconspicuous as he watched Ms. Sharper interact with her class. He figured that she must be somehow deviating from their common planning. He suspected she was doing something different to create a more positive atmosphere in her class.

He watched in disbelief as she taught her class. Instead of deviating from their planned lesson, she said almost the exact same words he had said many times that day. She did not alter instruction in any way that Mr. Jennings could see. Yet her students responded completely differently. They never asked whether the assignment was on the test or not. When she passed out the activity sheet, they didn't need to be told that it would be for a grade. Instead, her students began to work right away with enthusiasm.

Reaping What You Sow

When he sat down with her the next day, Mr. Jennings was bubbling over with questions. "How did you do it? I can't pass anything out to my students without them calculating the value of the assignment in relation to the test or their final grade. Do you forbid them to ask if it's for a grade? Should I do that too?"

Ms. Sharper responded slowly, "I never really thought about it. No, I haven't outlawed any questions. I just never really talk about the test or their class grades. I try to focus more on what we are learning and how it's useful for their lives."

Mr. Jennings thought about that for a moment. "I think you might be onto something. You never mentioned the semester exam or the weight of the assignment in the grade book. You just talked about how interesting the lesson was and related it to what they'd previously learned.

"As I think about my class, I don't think I go more than a day without mentioning the test. I know that getting good grades is important for many of these students fighting for college scholarships. I thought that stressing the importance of achieving well on the test would motivate them to try harder. It seems as if I've been shooting myself in the foot. While getting a good grade is important, it's not the most important thing. I guess my students care most about what they think I care most about."

Teachers Influence Goal Orientations

Whereas Day 22 focused on mastery goal orientation, the vignette today contrasted that with a performance goal orientation. Rather than valuing learning for learning's sake, some students place more value in achieving a goal. This mentality, called performance goal orientation, places more emphasis on achieving than learning.

While teachers do not have much say over the goal orientation students have when they enter their classroom, they can certainly change their views by the time they leave them. This area of motivational research is one of the most heavily studied and the evidence is decisive. Students who perceive that their classrooms have a mastery goal orientation are more likely to report using effective learning strategies. They use more higher-level thinking when knowledge, not achievement, is valued most by their teacher.

Additionally, teachers with a mastery goal orientation help their students prefer more challenging tasks. Rather than wanting an easy *A*, students will seek information and want to know more, even if that requires more effort. More than that, a mastery goal orientation environment increases students sense of competence. They are more apt to believe in the effectiveness of their effort if their teacher emphasizes the value of learning.

Assessment Practices

Creating an environment that values learning above achieving requires more than an occasional pep talk. Since tests are an integral part of the educational experience, they are a great place to start. Teachers can evaluate students in a way that supports a mastery goal orientation by making use of formative assessments. Normal classrooms tests taken as a grade are considered summative assessments. They come at the end of a unit and the information they provide about student mastery does not allow for improvement within the unit. Formative assessments, however, happen throughout a unit of study. Rather than being the final score, these interim tests act as benchmarks along the path toward a summative assessment. With this data, students can make adjustments to their learning before the final test.

Being shamed in front of one's peers is one of the most demoralizing things that can happen to a student. Students pay close attention to their social surroundings and public test scores affect them. Thus evaluation results, whether they be formative or summative, belong with the student and not with the class. Though posting test grades on the back wall is a quick way to give feedback, or you might think their display is motivational, it's actually counterproductive. Making evaluation results public reinforces a performance goal orientation.

If teachers use more formative assessments and praise the process rather than the product, bringing errors out of the shadows is another logical step. Too many times students hide their mistakes because they feel as if they are the only ones making them. By discussing mistakes and how students can learn from them, teachers can emphasize that errors are a normal part of learning.

References

Ames, C. (1992). Classrooms: Goals, structures, and student motivation. *Journal of Educational Psychology, 84*(3), 261.

Ames, C., & Archer, J. (1988). Achievement goals in the classroom: Students' learning strategies and motivational processes. *Journal of Educational Psychology, 80*(3), 260.

Elliot, A. J. (1999). Approach and avoidance motivation and achievement goals. *Educational Psychologist, 34*(3), 169-189.

Elliot, A. J., McGregor, H. A., & Gable, S. (1999). Achievement Goals, Study Strategies, and Exam Performance: A Mediational Analysis. *Journal of Educational Psychology, 91*(3), 549.

Linnenbrink, E. A. (2005). The Dilemma of Performance-Approach Goals: The Use of Multiple Goal Contexts to Promote Students' Motivation and Learning. *Journal of Educational Psychology, 97*(2), 197.

Day 23

Question: What type of goal orientation do your actions emphasize in your classroom? Do you place more value in learning or achieving? More importantly, how would your students answer those questions?

_____
_____
_____
_____
_____
_____
_____
_____
_____
_____

Action: If you do not already have one coming up, plan a formative assessment for your students. Let them know it's not for a grade but to help them understand what they know and what they have yet to learn. The experience of a non-graded test will be new for some students but repeated use of formative assessments will help encourage them to subconsciously move toward a mastery goal orientation.

Day 24: Performance Goal Orientation

When I entered college in 1996, I was basically a sophomore. I took several Advanced Placement (AP) courses in high school, was fortunate to pass all of the AP tests, and earned the equivalent of 20 college credits. I also was lucky enough to win a Presidential Merit Scholarship which provided me with the cost of full tuition at California Baptist University for four years. Yet with my credits entering college, it wouldn't take me the full four years to finish.

I started as any other freshman and took a full load of courses both semesters. My experience with dorm life in college was great and I enjoyed my time there. As I started to do the math my second year, I realized that progressing at a normal pace would put me in line to graduate early. I figured that there was no need to finish ahead of time. I decided to take the minimum number of courses I could to maintain my full-time status and spent an inordinate amount of hours playing Goldeneye 007 on my Nintendo 64 with my dorm mates. Those were the days.

Meeting the love of your life, however, tends to change things.

Summer Missionary

The summer after my first year of college, I worked at a camp in the mountains of California. I earned a minuscule stipend and free room and board for washing dishes for 10 weeks. I couldn't have been happier. The camp served as the training location for college students who came from all across the country to serve as summer missionaries to California. After two weeks of training, these students scattered across the state and helped with backyard Bible clubs and other projects.

The time it would take to do justice to the moment when my future wife walked into the room of the camp staff building is beyond the scope of a mere book chapter. Let me just summarize by saying that those moments in movies where two long-lost lovers see each other across a field of flowers and run in slow-motion toward each other with rising music in the background is based entirely on what happened that summer. It was literally love at first sight and we've been happily married ever since.

My kick-back, easy second year of college followed this summer encounter. I hated long-distance relationships but that girl from Fort Worth, TX was worth it. I was afraid not seeing each other for months at a time would ruin the relationship. We dated back in the dark ages when people wrote honest-to-goodness letters (the kinds that require a stamp) to each other. I was too broke to pay for long-distance telephone charges.

Graduation

Things steadily got more serious. By the end of my second year of college, we got engaged. It was then that I realized I had made a mistake with my lackadaisical approach to college enrollment. With the prospect of marriage and (gulp) adulthood looming, I quickly bored of college life. I wanted to be done with school, get married the following summer, and begin my working career. All that depended on graduating college, however, and I had damaged my prospects by taking it easy.

Determination, however, has never been in short supply with me. (My wife calls it mule-headed stubbornness, but it's just semantics). I calculated that in order to cram the remaining year and a half into my third year of college and graduate a year early, I would need to take 21 hours in the fall and 22 hours in the spring. This required special permission from the academic dean because anything more than 18 hours was considered unusual. In the spring, I had two required courses offered during the same time slot and I had to attend one and audit the other.

Needless to say, I was highly motivated. I didn't care so much about learning but about finishing. In addition, letting my grades slip was out of the question. I graduated college in three years, earned the school award for highest GPA, and got married two months after my graduation ceremony.

Performance Goal Orientation

While learning for learning's sake (mastery goal orientation) is the most beneficial, it's not the only thing that drives students to achieve. During my final year of college, I was highly motivated by a goal - graduating a year early so I could get married. That performance goal orientation drove me to take on a heavy workload and discipline myself more than I'd ever done in my life.

Students with a performance goal orientation typically have one of two desires. They either want to achieve a goal, called performance-approach, or they want to steer clear of an undesired outcome, called performance-avoidance. While the former can be just as motivating as mastery goal orientation, the latter is academically harmful.

Students who are motivated by a desire to avoid something, like failure or looking ignorant in front of their peers, use much more surface-level strategies. Their emotions are usually more negative and they achieve at a much lower rate than their performance-approach or mastery peers. Working to meet a goal or earn a recognition can be just as motivating as learning for its own sake. However, students who are driven by a fear of looking foolish or disappointing their parents are rarely successful.

Problem-based Learning

A widely used technique to increase the value of tasks is to ground them in the real world. Problem-based learning engages students by asking them to solve problems and/or develop products centered around real-world issues. Overall, there are six main types of problem-based learning.

1. *Systems analysis* asks students to examine the various parts and functions of a larger system.

2. *Problem solving* tasks have students identify an authentic problem for consideration.

3. *Historical investigations* require students to contemplate various situations, documents, and data from history.

4. *Invention* asks students to design a working product, presentation, or demonstration in response to a need.

5. *Experimental inquiry* uses the scientific method to design experiments to test hypotheses created by the students.

6. *Decision making* looks at a scenario and asks students to evaluate alternatives.

References

Elliot, A. J., McGregor, H. A., & Gable, S. (1999). Achievement Goals, Study Strategies, and Exam Performance: A Mediational Analysis. *Journal of Educational Psychology, 91*(3), 549.

Grant, H., & Dweck, C. S. (2003). Clarifying achievement goals and their impact. *Journal of Personality and Social Psychology, 85*(3), 541.

Liem, A. D., Lau, S., & Nie, Y. (2008). The role of self-efficacy, task value, and achievement goals in predicting learning strategies, task disengagement, peer relationship, and achievement outcome.

Contemporary Educational Psychology, 33(4), 486-512.

Linnenbrink, E. A. (2005). The Dilemma of Performance-Approach Goals: The Use of Multiple Goal Contexts to Promote Students' Motivation and Learning. *Journal of Educational Psychology, 97*(2), 197.

Pekrun, R., Elliot, A. J., & Maier, M. A. (2009). Achievement goals and achievement emotions: Testing a model of their joint relations with academic performance. *Journal of Educational Psychology, 101*(1), 115.

Silver, H. F., Strong, R. W., & Perini, M. J. (2007). *The strategic teacher: Selecting the right research-based strategy for every lesson.* ASCD.

Day 24

Question: When have you experienced a performance goal orientation? Did your desire to achieve something detract from your overall motivation?

_____
_____
_____
_____
_____
_____
_____
_____
_____
_____
_____

Action: Plan a problem-based learning task for an upcoming unit. Many online resources exist with ideas and even completed lessons around problem-based learning. Emphasize the relationship between the task and the real world.

Day 25: Different Performance Goals

Joshua and Phillip were discussing their latest assignment. The teacher had asked them to reflect on their feelings after the class spelling bee. They each had to write a short paragraph about the experience and what they learned from it. Both boys had studied for weeks but fell short in the end. Joshua finished in 2nd place and Phillip in 5th.

"I'm not sure why the teacher is asking us about our feelings," Phillip said. "I think the whole thing was a waste of time."

"What do you mean?" Joshua asked. "Weren't you excited about the spelling bee? We've been quizzing each other for the last week and I thought we had a good chance at winning."

"Yeah, but we didn't. We lost," Phillip replied. "I guess we're not as smart as we thought."

"I don't know. We did alright. You got 5th place. That's better than most of the class," Joshua said.

"Well, 5th isn't 2nd or 1st. I think spelling is stupid. Aren't you upset? You almost won! If it wasn't for that last word, you would be the champ," Phillip questioned.

Joshua thought about it for a minute. "No, I'm not mad. It would have been great to win but it was still fun to compete. I think next time I'll start studying a month before. The word I lost on was one at the end of the list I'd only seen a few times. We're having another spelling bee after Spring Break. Want to study together again?"

Phillip answered quickly. "No way. I'm not doing any more spelling bees. When I play, I play to win. Losing just makes me feel stupid. You can do it if you want but you'll have to find another study partner."

Reactions

Both boys thought about that silently and turned to their journals to complete their assignments. Phillip wrote that he didn't really like the spelling bee. He said that he didn't like looking foolish in front of his friends and that he wouldn't participate in the next one unless he had to. He spent a good portion of his reflection mulling over the words he was given to spell. Without coming right out and saying it, he felt that his words were harder than the ones given to the other students. He knew how to spell all the words his friends had to spell. For some reason, he felt, the most difficult ones had been saved for him.

Joshua's reflection was much different. He wrote about how exciting it was at the end of the spelling bee when it was just him and the eventual winner. Even though he lost in the end, his writing was generally upbeat. He said that he couldn't wait until the next one and that he was going to try to study harder so he could win. Rather than blaming his loss on the difficulty of the words he was given, he noted that he didn't put forth as much effort in preparing as he could have.

Different Performance Goals

Joshua and Phillip represent two different achievement goals that students exhibit in the classroom. Phillip's motivation revolves around his desire to validate his perceived ability. A type of performance goal orientation, students with ability goals want to be successful in what they do. They view tasks, projects, and competitions as a challenge to their intelligence. When successful, motivation is supported. In fact, solid performances increase their engagement and make them more eager to continue.

Yet that wasn't the case in the scenario. Phillip's lack of success had a negative outcome on his motivation. Even though his performance put him in the top tier of his class, he still used the loss to support his belief in his lack of ability. Those with ability goal orientations can feel an increased sense of helplessness after a failure. They experience a loss of self-worth, tend to ruminate more about the setback, and lose intrinsic motivation. Ultimately, this will lead to decreased achievement.

Joshua valued a different performance goal. Rather than trying to validate his own ability, the desire to beat his classmates drove his actions. Called a normative goal, this other type of performance goal focuses more on outperforming others. Even though he didn't win, Joshua enjoyed the thrill of the hunt. Normative goals have not been shown to generate a feeling of helplessness when encountering setbacks. Neither do they cause students to lose intrinsic motivation.

Reflections

A simple technique that teachers can use to motivate students is to ask them to reflect. Usually written, though sometimes oral or mental, reflections encourage students to evaluate many parts of their learning. Students can examine their thought processes, motivation, goal orientation, and even effort. The scenario highlighted an example of using a reflection to ask students to indirectly think about their goal orientation.

Another type of reflection is a progress reflection. Students gauge how close they are to meeting the desired outcomes of the lesson or unit. Also, teachers can ask students to reflect on their effort. Did they push through obstacles on their way to learning or were they mentally coasting? Did they give it their best or did they do the bare minimum?

Finally, for teachers that utilize group learning, students can reflect on their contributions to the group and how well the group worked as a team. Rather than chiding students for behavior that is detrimental to group learning, allow them an opportunity to evaluate their role in the group's performance.

If students are stuck in a reflective rut, consider these questions based on Bloom's Taxonomy:

- Remembering: What did I do?
- Understanding: What was important about it?
- Applying: Where could I use this again?
- Analyzing: Do I see any patterns in what I did?
- Evaluating: How well did I do?
- Creating: What should I do next?

References

Grant, H., & Dweck, C. S. (2003). Clarifying achievement goals and their impact. *Journal of Personality and Social Psychology, 85*(3), 541.

Pappas, P. (2010, January 4). *A Taxonomy of Reflection: Critical Thinking For Students, Teachers, and Principals (Part 1)*. Retrieved March 15, 2017, from http://peterpappas.com/2010/01/taxonomy-reflection-critical-thinking-students-teachers-principals-.html

Day 25

Question: Think about your target student. Do you feel his/her motivation is more ability-based (like Phillip) or more normative-based (like Joshua)? Consider his/her reaction to setbacks as a guide.

_____

_____

_____

_____

_____

_____

_____

_____

_____

_____

Action: Build a reflection into an upcoming lesson. Instead of assigning a typical worksheet, ask students to gauge how close they are to meeting the lesson outcomes. You'll be surprised at the honesty of student answers.

DAY 26: DEVELOPING INTEREST

Ever since I was a child I've enjoyed playing sports. I played baseball in city leagues and basketball after school with my friends. I even joined the tennis team my freshman year of high school. While I liked the thrill of competition, sometimes practicing was too much work. Baseball requires many people to get anything like an organized game going. Basketball can be played with just a few people or even practiced alone. Tennis is nice because it only requires one other person to play.

Yet the problem was, I wasn't very good. Don't get me wrong, I could play. I just wasn't great. I was lucky if I made it to the middle of the pack on any team I played for. Like most kids, I enjoyed winning more than losing. The older I got, though, the more I realized that in order to be great, I would need to focus all of my energy on one thing. Rather than being a jack-of-all-trades athlete, I'd have to pick a sport and give it my all. To reach the highest levels, I would need to dedicate my life to becoming the best.

I just wasn't that interested. That required too much effort. I stopped playing sports after my freshman year and turned more to academics. While I had the capacity to earn good grades, I never lost my love of sports. What I needed was a sport that I could play by myself. If I could challenge myself and rate myself against personal goals, it wouldn't be so evident that I was mediocre. I could have fun without having my vanilla-ness shoved in my face by hardcore athletes.

Thankfully, my brother came to my rescue.

Disc Golf

Several years ago, our families got together for Christmas at his house in Mississippi. As an afternoon diversion, he took us out to a local state park to play disc golf. I'd tossed a Frisbee or two around as a child but had no real idea about what disc golf was. I knew about regular golf (once again, I played it some but was never any good at it) and figured this was a knock-off version. I couldn't have been more wrong.

That day at Lake Lowndes State Park began a passion in me that borders on obsession (according to my wife, at least). What I initially thought of as chucking a disc around the woods turned out to be a highly technical and physical sport. The intricacies of disc design, throwing techniques, and specialty shots is beyond the scope of this chapter. Needless to say, I would highly recommend disc golf to anyone. What has intrigued me the most, however, is that my interest in the game has grown over the years.

While I always liked it, I kept waiting for it to die off like any other sport I played. I knew I would never be as good as professional players on PDGA tour (yes, that's a thing). Instead of losing interest, though, it grew. From time to time I'll play with some friends from church but usually I play on my own. Every once in a while I'll even watch some YouTube videos to try and improve an aspect of my game, such as putting or driving. It wasn't until recently that I finally figured out why disc golf stuck when so many other sports I played fell by the wayside.

Developing Interest

Interest in a task depends on positive feedback in two areas - cognitive and emotional. When those conditions are met, interest develops. With my continued experiences with disc golf, interest has been growing for years. On the cognitive side, the rules of the game make sense to me. I understand the uses of various discs and when forehand shots are more appropriate. My previous knowledge of golf made it a seamless transition to pick up the nuances of disc golf.

More importantly, though, disc golf is fun! The emotional feedback I get is very positive. I can challenge myself on courses, trying to make perfect shots and relishing the occasional birdies. While I do play some with others, I don't play with semi-professionals. When I lose, it's close and I'm encouraged to keep trying. There is always a light at the end of the competitive tunnel.

I tried to get my oldest son Dave interested awhile back. I could only convince him to play a few times before he gave it up. The strange thing is, he has more natural aptitude for it than I do. His throws are much straighter and regular than my herky-jerky movements. Yet he never enjoyed playing with me because I always beat him. My additional experience and ability to throw farther put him at a disadvantage. That lack of positive emotional feedback kept him from ever developing a lasting interest in the game.

Create Confusion

There are many ways to help students develop interest in learning. One way, which might seem oxymoronic at first, is to confuse them. Too many times teachers over simplify the material students need to learn. They do all the cognitive heavy lifting and then spoon-feed the information to the class. If used correctly, confusion can be an important emotion for learning.

Known in research circles as cognitive disequilibrium, confusion happens when students are engaged in an activity or task and become stuck. They might encounter an obstacle to a goal, an interruption of organized action sequences, or even contradictions. Somehow, things are going along smoothly and then they hit a mental speed bump. It's this confusion that can be a springboard to deeper learning.

The mental impasse demands a solution. As the brain seeks to return to a balanced state, the student is actively trying to figure out the solution to the problem. If the roadblock is resolved satisfactorily, cognitive equilibrium reemerges. The task is continued but now at a deeper level. Figuring out how to overcome the obstacle created a new understanding for the student. If teachers can harness this, they can further engage students by making them work for answers.

See the image titled *Crazy Math* as an example. After an initial glance, something should seem off and you should experience a moment (or three) of confusion. The first equation makes perfect sense but the second and third don't quite compute (literally). Add to that the text which describes this problem as "crazy math" and viola, a cognitive roadblock. Once you figure out the answer, your understanding of the answer will be much deeper than if I simply told you what to do. (Hint – the answer is NOT 40. *Solution is on the next page).

Crazy Math

$1 + 4 = 5$

$2 + 5 = 12$

$3 + 6 = 21$

$8 + 11 = ?$

Figure 3: Crazy Math

References

Hidi, S., & Renninger, K. A. (2006). The four-phase model of interest development. *Educational Psychologist, 41*(2), 111-127.

Krapp, A. (1999). Interest, motivation and learning: An educational-psychological perspective. *European Journal of Psychology and Education, 14*(1), 23-40.

Krapp, A. (2006). Basic needs and the development of interest and intrinsic motivational orientations. *Learning and Instruction, 15*(5), 381-395.

Shernoff, D. J., Csikszentmihalyi, M., Shneider, B., & Shernoff, E. S. (2003). Student engagement in high school classrooms from the perspective of flow theory. *School Psychology Quarterly, 18*(2), 158.

*Multiply the second addend by the first addend and then add the first addend to the product. So, 1×4+1=5, 2×5+2=12, 3×6+3=21, and **8×11+8=96**.

Day 26

Question: When have you been interested in learning something and when has your interest dried up? What do you think caused the difference in your engagement?

_____
_____
_____
_____
_____
_____
_____
_____
_____
_____

Action: Think of an upcoming lecture or time of direct instruction. Instead of telling the students what they need to know, design a task or problem that causes initial confusion. Help students push through the cognitive roadblocks and develop deeper understanding.

Day 27: Sustained Interest

Being interested in something sometimes makes you do the strangest things. My second oldest son, Drew, is currently in the 8th grade. He has participated in band since he entered middle school three years ago. He absolutely loves it and has a natural aptitude for the bassoon. As much as he loves making music, hanging out with his friends, and doing something well, there is one part of band he hates.

Practicing.

In support of the band teacher, my wife and I would remind Drew every day to practice when he got home from school. It's absolutely amazing how motivated he became to find other things to do. At times, he would develop an unexplained headache that would last until dinner, making him unable to practice. Sometimes he would claim he had homework, though he usually never did have any and rarely got away with that excuse.

His favorite (and our least favorite) effort to avoid practicing was saying he had to go to the bathroom. While that might seem innocent to you, the reader, it was actually a nefarious plot to undermine the stability of our family unit. First, we only have one bathroom in our house for six people. (The sixth person, Daniel, is still in diapers, but it's the principle of the matter). Second, using the restroom and then vacating the room would not be a problem.

However, his trips to the bathroom turned into 30 minute odysseys during which he hogged the toilet and no one else could use it. Naturally, our other two other children would be fine until he went in there. Suddenly their bowels would turn to mush, their bladders shriveled to the size of a pea, and all because Drew didn't want to practice the bassoon.

Finally, this year, Drew's 8th grade schedule allowed him an extra period of band during the day. He now practices during that additional period and our toilet rotation has finally returned to normal. Which is why it was so strange when Drew came home in October with another instrument and started practicing. On his own. Without prompting. Every day. For weeks.

The high school he'll attend next year has a fantastic band program. Specifically, their marching band has a very successful performance record and consistently competes in the state UIL competition. For those who have played in band, you might know where this is going. Drew loves band. He's going to continue playing band all throughout high school and, hopefully, it'll even earn him a few scholarships for college.

You can't play bassoon in a marching band.

Marching Band

During one of the last high school football games in the fall, the 8th graders were going to join the high school band on the field during halftime and play a song. For the 8th graders, it was a dream come true. For Drew to participate, however, he had to learn a new instrument. His band teacher gave him a saxophone a few weeks before the game to play. Honestly, he probably would have been fine if Drew had just walked out there with the instrument and stood there. But not Drew.

His interest in learning a new instrument, and participating in the halftime song, drove him to do the unthinkable - practice at home. The two instruments are different on several levels. First and foremost, bassoon is a double-reed instrument while the saxophone uses a single reed. The way each fits and feels in the mouth is entirely unique. The fingerings for notes are very different. The saxophone also requires more air to produce sound.

Drew had enough band experience to quickly pick up the new instrument and play. He wasn't interested in being a field decoration, however. He wanted to play every note that the other saxophones were playing. Drew practiced and practiced daily until it sounded like an instrument and not the slaughter of an elk in mating season. Within weeks, he picked up a new instrument and learned to play it adequately. He participated in the song at halftime and had a blast. Consequently, we haven't seen or heard the saxophone since.

Sustained Interest

Interest is developed when we received positive feedback from an activity, both cognitive and emotional. Sustained interest, though, has many benefits, as exhibited in the story of Drew and the saxophone. Students with sustained interest show increased attention. They have a greater ability to direct their thoughts and focus on the task at hand, even for long periods of time.

In addition, sustained interest increases recall of information. When something truly captures the attention of students, their entire focus is on that subject. The amount of information they receive is enhanced, and more importantly, the volume of information they remember is also affected. If students can't remember a lesson you taught a week ago, there's a good chance it didn't generate enough interest.

Finally, sustained interest increases persistence. As long as students are receiving the positive emotional and cognitive feedback, running into obstacles won't stop them. They'll fight through until they solve whatever problem arises. On the other hand, students will little to no interest in an activity will allow minor setbacks to stop their learning. If they don't have enough interest, they'll take any excuse to stop.

Beneficial Bickering

While most teachers try their hardest to keep arguments out of the classroom, they might just provide excellent opportunities to engage the interest of students. Our brains naturally are drawn to controversy and our attention ratchets up when something spectacular happens. Think about the collective "oooohhhhh" that usually occurs when a student talks back to a teacher and the class knows that the student is about to get in some serious trouble.

Helpful arguments, then, ask students to take a position on something and then defend it. This naturally piques the interest of students as they fight to maintain their reasoning in the face of opposition. This can result in increased positive feelings if handled responsibly.

A common form of beneficial bickering is the use of debates. Students form two groups to debate both sides of an argument. The focus is on use of evidence and persuasion. Each side should prepare an opening statement, be allowed to question the opposing side, and then provide a rebuttal and/or closing argument.

Since the purpose is to more deeply understand the content (rather than just letting the students argue), the key to using debates is the synthesis component after both sides have concluded their arguments. Students should then decide upon a position, regardless of the position they argued during the debate, and defend it with reasoning and evidence. Teachers can also ask students to reflect on the debate itself and rate their participation and whether or not students kept things positive and professional.

References

Ainley, M., Hidi, S., & Berndorff, D. (2002). Interest, learning, and the psychological processes that mediate their relationship. *Journal of Educational Psychology, 94*(3), 545.

Hidi, S., & Renninger, K. A. (2006). The four-phase model of interest development. *Educational Psychologist, 41*(2), 111-127.

Immordino-Yang, M. H., & Damasio, A. (2007). We feel, therefore we learn: The relevance of affective and social neuroscience to education. *Mind, Brain, and Education, 1*(1), 3-10.

Krapp, A. (1999). Interest, motivation and learning: An educational-psychological perspective. *European Journal of Psychology and Education, 14*(1), 23-40.

Pekrun, R., Goetz, T. T., & Perry, R. P. (2002). Academic emotions in students' self-regulated learning and achievement: A program of qualitative and quantitative research. *Educational Psychologist, 37*(2), 91-105.

Shernoff, D. J., Csikszentmihalyi, M., Shneider, B., & Shernoff, E. S. (2003). Student engagement in high school classrooms from the perspective of flow theory. *School Psychology Quarterly, 18*(2), 158.

Day 27

Question: When have you seen a sustained interest in your students? What were they learning that increased their attention, recall, and persistence?

_____

_____

_____

_____

_____

_____

_____

_____

_____

_____

Action: Look at an upcoming assignment and find a question that has more than one right answer (e.g., an opinion question). Plan on letting students debate the question, either in small groups or as an entire class. Allow them time to prepare their arguments and ask for a final answer from students after they've heard both sides of the debate.

Day 28: Emotions Matter

"Suck it up! Dry your tears!"

I'm going to have a hard time getting those words out of my mind. I heard them come from a very successful educational leader at a recent conference. At this leader's school, crying is not tolerated. When students grow frustrated, tired, or break down in any other way, they are told to suck it up. There's no crying at that school.

The leader touted the fact that after a few days, the students usually stopped crying. After being told this repeatedly by the staff of the school, the students figured out that crying won't make it any easier. Instead, they pushed through their problems and became more resilient. This leader is nationally recognized in the field of education. Teachers and principals from all over the world come to bask in the awesomeness of the school, which has phenomenal results.

Unfortunately, they're going about it all wrong.

School? No Thank You

Emotions affect everything we do. For most students, they aren't optional or controllable. Their developing minds and bodies have little control over their actions, let alone their thoughts or emotions. When my son Drew entered the first grade many years ago, I had already been a teacher for almost a decade. Needless to say, I thought I knew just about everything I needed to know about children. Between being a father and a teacher, I saw students from both perspectives.

Drew had a great first grade teacher. She was fun, innovative, and truly loved her students. For sensitive six-year-olds, she was exactly was needed to guide them through the difficulties of handwriting, phonics, and learning how to line up properly. Drew loved his teacher and we still have a relationship with her and her family seven years later. Yet Drew hated going to school.

My wife and I could never figure out what the deal was. For some reason, he started whining and whimpering when my wife told him it was time to go to school. He would run from her, complain of a tummy ache, whatever he could think of. We knew that he liked his teacher. He had many friends in the class and it was a positive learning atmosphere. He just didn't want to go to school. As both a father and an educator, I was stumped.

A Caring Response

Every morning my wife would begin the routine and eventually convince him to get in the car. As they pulled up to the school, another battle ensued trying to get him out of the vehicle. Most mornings, he would finally get out and trudge up to the front door. Sometimes he would still be crying as he marched toward his perceived doom. The worst was when he would turn and give my wife that look that dogs give their owners when they know they're being taken to the pound.

It usually took him about fifteen minutes to pull himself together. Sometimes he'd sit with the counselor, sometimes at the back of his classroom. If neither option was available, he'd sit with the secretary in the front office until his emotions got under control. He wasn't angry or depressed. Drew didn't throw a fit or even demand to go home. He was just sad, most likely suffering a bit from separation anxiety. Once he had a chance to sit for a bit, he'd feel better. He would go to his class and fully participate. When my wife would pick him up in the afternoon, he'd say he had a great day at school. Yet it would start again the next morning.

The school handled Drew's emotions wonderfully. If they had decided to toughen him up, however, and tell him to dry up his tears, he would have been irreparably harmed. When he was in an agitated emotional state, he couldn't think through his feelings and understand that his caring teacher was waiting for him with open arms. He was too busy emoting to have any rational thought.

Plus, if someone has told Drew to suck it up, I think my wife would have committed a felony. Or worse.

Emotions Matter

Emotions serve as the gatekeeper to learning. They affect almost every part of cognition and rather than being ignored or patronized, they should be recognized as an essential part of who we are. First and foremost, emotions affect the use of learning strategies. When students are in a positive emotional state, they'll use deeper, more conceptual learning strategies.

Emotions also affect students' ability to regulate their thoughts and behavior. When in the thrall of an emotional outburst, students have difficulty keeping calm and reasonable. More than that, learning is the furthest thing from their minds. They are not able to organize their thoughts, think through their actions, or plan for the future. Telling them to dry their tears usually doesn't help.

Finally, and most importantly to educators, emotions affect academic performance. In general, positive emotions predict a far better performance than negative emotions. When students are in a bad mood, ignoring or minimizing it won't make it go away. In fact, that mood might make it harder for them to learn.

Emotional Anchors

Have you ever seen a movie that was completely forgettable? Sometimes my wife and I will start watching a movie only to realize that we've seen it before. One reason we couldn't remember it because it never connected with us emotionally. Ask people about *Star Wars*, *Braveheart*, *Lord of the Rings*, or *Inception*, though, and people can still talk about specific plot points (or holes) even if they haven't seen it in ten years. For me, the juxtaposition of hormonal imbalances in high school and *Dumb and Dumber* has irrevocably changed who I am as a person.

Take a historically boring subject, grammar, for example. Successful writing teachers find emotional tie-ins for their students in order to make grammar memorable and transferrable to personal writing. Some ditch all their worksheets (a move I applaud) and base all instruction on the students' writing. Through the emotions usually encountered when truly creating writing of one's own accord (as opposed to responding robotically to prompts passed out on worksheets), teachers can leverage the emotional power of writing itself to work on improving word choice, subject-verb agreement, and sentence structure. Other teachers make the learning of grammar rules themselves fun by incorporating mnemonics, raps, or other techniques designed to elicit emotional connectivity.

Learning can (and should) be fun. By increasing positive emotions and using those to anchor knowledge, student participation and achievement will also increase.

References

Goetz, T., Pekrun, R., Hall, N., & Haag, L. (2006). Academic emotions from a social-cognitive perspective: Antecedents and domain specificity of students' affect in the context of Latin instruction. *British Journal of Educational Psychology, 76*(2), 289-308.

Hidi, S., & Renninger, K. A. (2006). The four-phase model of interest development. *Educational Psychologist, 41*(2), 111-127.

Krapp, A. (1999). Interest, motivation and learning: An educational-psychological perspective. *European Journal of Psychology and Education, 14*(1), 23-40.

Pekrun, R. (2006). The control-value theory of achievement emotions: Assumptions, corollaries, and implications for educational research and practice. *Educational Psychology Review, 18*(4), 315-341.

Pekrun, R., Elliot, A. J., & Maier, M. A. (2009). Achievement goals and achievement emotions: Testing a model of their joint relations with academic performance. *Journal of Educational Psychology, 101*(1), 115.

Pekrun, R., Goetz, T. T., & Perry, R. P. (2002). Academic emotions in students' self-regulated learning and achievement: A program of qualitative and quantitative research. *Educational Psychologist, 37*(2), 91-105.

Pekrun, R., Goetz, T., Frenzel, A. C., Barchfeld, P., & Perry, R. P. (2011). Measuring emotions in students' learning and performance: The Achievement Emotions Questionnaire (AEQ). *Contemporary Educational Psychology, 36*(1), 36-48.

Day 28

Question: Think of your target student. When s/he is in a bad mood, how is learning affected? Does telling him/her to calm down usually work?

_____
_____
_____
_____
_____
_____
_____
_____
_____
_____

Action: Look at your upcoming lessons and focus on what you consider the most boring part for an emotional anchor. Take that content and make it fun! Create a rhyme or mnemonic. Make a game students can play to cover the content. Inject some positive emotions and watch the learning grow.

Day 29: Emotions Affect Creativity

There were three factors that inspired me to research student motivation and eventually write a book. I discussed my encounter with Jenny on Day 22 and my son Dave's complete lack of enthusiasm on Day 21. While those events certainly caused me to ask some questions, they didn't provide the emotional boost needed to start such daunting task. The third factor happened when I almost lost my son before he was born.

The doctor came in for his normal check of my wife's progress, who was in labor with our fourth child. He discovered that Daniel had his umbilical cord wrapped around his neck twice. Additionally, a loop of it was hanging down below him. In less than a minute after the doctor declared, "We need to do an emergency C-section, now!", my wife was in surgery. I numbly followed the bed as it rolled away, wondering what had just happened.

As we both waited anxiously for the operation to finish and to hear the cry, time seemed to slow. Heather later told me she knew he had been taken from her womb, yet we had heard nothing. The silence was truly deafening.

The Cry

After an eternity of silence interrupted by whirring and beeping, we heard a piteous wail. We looked into each other's eyes and both smiled in relief. But that one cry was all we heard. Rather than a raucous entry into the world trumpeted with healthy screeching, Daniel gave one tepid whimper and then became silent again.

One of the scrubbed medical professionals came around the blue sheet. He asked me if I wanted to see my son. As I walked around the partition, a new tableau opened before my eyes. Four nurses were surrounding an elevated crib under a heat lamp. As I moved closer and looked over their shoulders, I saw Daniel. His skin had a blue tint and he was just barely breathing. As his chest rose and fell incrementally, one of the nurses, alternately rubbing his feet and gently slapping him, repeated the phrase, "Come on little guy, breathe. Come on, breathe."

When asked if I wanted to stay with my wife or go with my son upstairs, who was immediately transferred to the Neonatal Intensive Care Unit (NICU), my heart was ripped in half. I looked at Heather and without a word we both knew what I had to do, what she would do in my place. I left her prone on the surgical table, waiting to be sewn up by her doctor, surrounded by faceless strangers in blue masks.

Gratitude

Gratitude overcame me as I thought of the people working in NICU that Saturday evening. After an endless three minutes of mandatory hand washing, I found my son amidst a tangle of wires, monitors, and cords. Those next few days blended together into one endless series of nurses checking on my wife, walking with her slowly to NICU every few hours to feed Daniel, and praying. Eventually he pulled through. After a rough start, my son turned the corner and we came home four days later.

It was during one of those slow walks with my wife to NICU that a thought hit me which served as a turning point in my life. As Daniel seemed to be improving and my wife spent her days sleeping and walking back and forth from NICU, I was able to reflect more on my profession. My gratitude for the doctors and nurses who acted and to save my son's life nagged at me like waves rolling onto a bleak shore. Their jobs, dealing with life and death, made me feel small and insignificant.

The Power of an Educator

Then a truth slammed into me – I am an educator. I work to save lives every day. Children come to me from broken homes, abused and hungry, and look to me for life. I teach them to read, to write, to perform mathematical calculations. I teach them to take turns, to be a good friend, to work hard, and to share. From me, I hope they learn about endurance, problem-solving, and self-efficacy. When no one else does, I believe in them. I am their hero, their role model, their advocate.

That moment was wiped away, though, by the precision, concentration, and assuredness of the doctors and nurses I saw. Through rigorous training, education, and experience, they work endlessly to achieve their goal. They determine what is standing in the way of that target and relentlessly pursue the patient's well-being regardless of the obstacles thrown at them. Focused, equipped, and highly efficient are good descriptors of their professionalism.

I wish that I could use those same adjectives to describe the schools I've worked at and the classrooms in which I've taught. It was this stark realization that crystalized the need for more information. It was the emotional trauma of my son's birth, plus the continuing issues with Dave and the memory of my failure with Jenny, that combined to push me to learn more. If no one else could create a framework for student motivation, I'd just have to do it myself.

Emotions Affect Creativity

Positive emotional states enhance creativity. In other words, feeling good can inspire students. When teachers complain about the lack of originality in their students' work, they might look to their moods. People with negative feelings have a much harder time being creative.

I had enough reason from Dave and Jenny to start researching a subject I wanted to know more about. Yet the drive to create meaning from a random series of academic research articles didn't come until my son Daniel was born. The emotional roller coaster I went through and my gratitude toward those medical professionals inspired me to try and make my own contribution to helping children.

Additionally, emotions are essential for efficient decision-making. Some might think that cold logic is the best foundation for making choices. However, research with brain-damaged individuals shows that not being able to access emotions greatly harms the decisions people make. We rely as much on our feelings as we do on reason when deciding what to do.

Incorporate Movement

Movement for learning positively affects the emotions of students by getting them up and out of their seats. One example of this is to place group work in various corners of the classroom. Instead of the traditional practice problems that students and groups work through at their desks, each problem can be placed in a corner of the classroom. In order to complete the problems, students need to rotate around the room, thus adding a little movement to ordinary learning tasks.

Hand motions are a great way to put small movements into any lesson while also improving learning. Whether they are teacher-created or student-created, almost anything can be enhanced with hand motions. For example, students learning the order of operations in mathematics can associate a movement with each to cement learning into their minds.

- Parentheses – Hold arms down at their sides, slightly bent and bulging out

- Exponent – Use hands to form a circle held next to the left ear

- Multiplication and Division – Make an X shape with both arms and then hold arms parallel to each other with closed fists to represent division

- Addition and Subtraction – Use both arms to make a cross sign and then take the vertical arm away to represent subtraction

References

Immordino-Yang, M. H. (2011). Implications of affective and social neuroscience for educational theory. *Educational Philosophy and Theory, 43*(1), 98-103.

Immordino-Yang, M. H., & Damasio, A. (2007). We feel, therefore we learn: The relevance of affective and social neuroscience to education. *Mind, Brain, and Education, 1*(1), 3-10.

Isen, A. M. (2001). An influence of positive affect on decision making in complex situations: Theoretical issues with practical implications. *Journal of Consumer Psychology, 11*(2), 75-85.

Pekrun, R., Goetz, T. T., & Perry, R. P. (2002). Academic emotions in students' self-regulated learning and achievement: A program of qualitative and quantitative research. *Educational Psychologist, 37*(2), 91-105.

Day 29

Question: Think about the last time you felt really creative. What were your emotions like at the time? Do you think you could have accomplished the same creative output if you were angry or depressed?

_____

_____

_____

_____

_____

_____

_____

_____

_____

Action: Take something you are teaching in the near future and incorporate some movement into the lesson. Use hand motions, have the students move to various parts of the room, or even bring in some dance moves. You can also ask students to work together to make their own movements for the content.

Day 30: Negative Emotions Harm Learning

The boys got their papers back and compared their scores. Not one of them passed but their teacher, Mr. Demasio, allowed them to redo it for up to a 70 if they corrected their mistakes. In addition, he told the class that he wanted them to write a short paragraph explaining why they think they failed. The boys could figure out the right answers by working together but why they failed varied.

"What are you going to put, Greg?" Anthony asked. "Why did you fail?"

Greg responded right away. "I know what my problem was. I was bored and wasn't really paying attention. When Mr. Demasio teaches science it's usually my favorite class. We do all kinds of experiments and learn cool stuff. Math is boring. All we do is worksheets and multiplication problems. I wish math had experiments like science."

Anthony disagreed, "I don't know it. I wouldn't say it's boring. I just stink at math."

"What do you mean? You're one of the fastest students when we have math facts challenges!" Jeff piped in.

"Well, math facts challenges are one thing. They're just for fun. If I mess up, it doesn't really matter. Tests are more serious. My parents always tell me that I have to earn straight As. They're going to flip out when they see this score. Even getting it up to a 70 won't make them happy," Anthony complained.

"You just need to chill out, man," Greg advised.

"Chill out? No way," Anthony said. "These tests are a big deal. I just start to freak out when it's the real thing. I do alright on homework and classwork but tests make me start to sweat. What about you, Jeff?"

Anger

"I don't know. Usually I do okay but I got in a fight with my brother that morning," Jeff said. "He came into my room without permission, like he always does, but this time wearing my gaming headphones. I've told him about a million times not to wear them because they're expensive. He dances around my room with them on and steps on the cord.

"The next thing I know, he's tripped over the cord, fell into the bed rail, and cut his cheek. The headphones flew off and crashed into the wall, cracking one whole side. I start screaming at him for messing around with my headphones and then my mom walks in. She sees the blood on his cheek and starts to yell at me. She didn't even care that he broke my headphones.

"I was still angry when I took the test. I probably could have gotten a better score but I just hate how my parents always stick up for my little brother," Jeff finished.

The friends sat quietly, thinking about their own parents and siblings. Finally, Jeff looked over at Murray. "Hey, man, what about you? What you going to write for Mr. Demasio?"

Hopelessness

Murray mumbled something that his friends couldn't hear. When they asked him to say it again, he said a little louder, "It won't do any good."

Greg asked, "What do you mean?"

"I can't do it. I don't know how to fix any of my answers," Murray said.

"We'll help you, man," the boys said. "We're going to work on our answers together."

"Yeah, but it won't help. I can't do math. I still use my fingers when adding. I've almost failed math every year. I had to go to summer school last year just to pass for the year. No matter what I do, there are too many steps. It never makes any sense," Murray sighed.

The bell rang and the boys split up, thinking about what they would write for Mr. Demasio. It was a sad group without uncertain hopes of future success.

Negative Emotions Harm Learning

Students who experience negative emotions, such as boredom, anxiety, anger, or hopelessness, use more surface-level processing. While their cognitive abilities might not be impaired, their emotional distress gets in the way of learning. In the vignette, Greg exhibited the effects of boredom. Math never really caught his attention and his grades suffered. While he enjoyed science, mathematics always seemed tedious. His learning, as a result, was more passive and surface-level.

Anthony's feeling of anxiety has been heavily researched over the years. Students who feel anxious, especially about tests, do much worse than their peers. The additional pressure they put on themselves to perform is actually counterproductive. Jeff's problem, anger, also affected his performance. Even though his dilemma didn't directly relate to math, his emotional state at the time of the test made it harder for him to perform normally.

Murray's feeling of helplessness is a common problem for students who have failed in the past. For many, motivation is hard to come by because they do not feel competent. That feeling of intellectual impotence causes students to feel hopeless and drains student motivation. Overall, negative emotions harm learning in students. They cause students to use more surface-level processing techniques and correlate to lower performance.

Novelty

Change things up! One way to pique interest and help generate positive emotions in students is to stay out of a rut. What you consider establishing a routine might in fact create a sense of boredom. Try some of these ideas to take a normal activity and inject a new twist into it.

- Have students get up and take three steps in any direction. After the three steps, have them freeze and chat with the closest two students about what they just learned.

- Tell corny jokes. Get a joke book or two and keep them handy. Infuse them into the lesson or tell them at random times.

- Cut out great comic strips from the Sunday paper and share them with the students. The humor is usually pretty sophisticated and can generate some great conversations about figurative language and drawing conclusions.

- Use music! Students love listening to music, making music, and sharing their favorite songs. As long as the lyrics are appropriate, different students can serve as DJ for the day and select which songs to play during individual work time.

- Having students work on daily challenges is another great way to mix things up. Teachers can pull many different types of challenges from brain teaser or logic books/websites. These challenges should be focused, done with a group, and not graded.

- Change the verbal dynamics. Have students talk with a partner about the content without using any proper nouns or in the third person. Have them act out a summary of what they learned while not using any words at all.

- Incorporate various call-and-response phrases. For example, students can be trained to say, "Same size, same shape" whenever the teacher uses the word "congruent" in a sentence.

References

D'Mello, S., & Graesser, A. (2012). Dynamics of affective states during complex learning. *Learning and Instruction, 22*(2), 145-157.

Pekrun, R. (2006). The control-value theory of achievement emotions: Assumptions, corollaries, and implications for educational research and practice. *Educational Psychology Review, 18*(4), 315-341.

Pekrun, R., Goetz, T. T., & Perry, R. P. (2002). Academic emotions in students' self-regulated learning and achievement: A program of qualitative and quantitative research. *Educational Psychologist, 37*(2), 91-105.

Day 30

Question: When students are exhibiting negative emotions, do you comfort them or expect them to continue learning like normal? How does your reaction affect their performance?

_____

_____

_____

_____

_____

_____

_____

_____

_____

_____

Action: Use novelty to spark a little enthusiasm in your class. Take a routine task and do it in a different way to increase interest among your students.

Afterward

Breathe!

You made it through the thirty-day journey and learned many new things along the way. You now have the CRAVE model of student motivation as a foundation for your understanding of learning behavior. Moving forward, use the five facets as a filter through which you can assess the motivational needs of your students.

This book is more than simply a diagnostic tool, however. Within these pages are many suggestions, thoughts, and ideas which would be difficult to implement in a year, let alone in 30 days. Give yourself permission to try out a few things at a time and not feel pressured to do everything at once. It's better to do a few things well than many things poorly.

Time will fade the specifics within these pages. After a year or so, make a point of flipping through them again. You'll find that a new set of students will bring a new set of challenges. What did not seem relevant during your first time through the book might jump out as extremely helpful when considering different students.

May all your students crave learning!

Appendix 1: CRAVE Review of Literature

Below is a recap of the major educational psychology theories (in no particular order) used to describe motivation as it pertains to the classroom setting. My purpose in summarizing these ideas is to communicate them to the average adult. Thus, there are places in which paraphrasing is used to avoid an overabundance of technical jargon.

Expectancy-Value Theory

The first formal expectancy-value model described people's motivation in achievement situations. It believed that what caused student behaviors was determined by an individual's achievement motives, expectancies for success, and incentive values (Wigfield & Eccles, 1992). Other researchers have built on this model, both expanding it and personalizing it for their own studies. Bernard Weiner (1985) proposed the attributional theory (discussed below) to explain what impacts student expectancies for success. A widely-used variation of this model has been most heavily researched by Wigfield and Eccles (2000). It theorizes that both expectancies, which are influenced by ability beliefs along with the perceived difficulty of the task and individual goals, and values, including attainment values (importance of doing well), intrinsic values, perceived usefulness of the task, and cost (both effort and emotional), are key factors in determining a student's motivation. Adding to this, Pintrich and De Groot (1990) adapted the model to include a third component, affective or emotional.

To sum up, the expectancy-value model describes student motivation as being subject to two major dimensions. The first, expectancy, contains beliefs of competence, self-efficacy, and goal orientation. In other words, students are more motivated if they think they can perform adequately and expect success from an activity or task. The second dimension is value, which contains attainment values, utility values, and expected effort. Student motivation, then, is also seen to be influenced by how valuable the task is to the student and if the task is worth the effort needed to complete it. The expectancy-value model theorizes that how motivated a child is to perform a task depends on the degree to which the child expects success and how much value the child places in the activity.

For example, a student may be a whiz at multiplication facts but believe them worthless or unrelated to her world, resulting in low motivation to engage in the task. Another student might love history and binge watches the History channel but be horrible with remembering dates and timelines, thus is uninterested in filling out a worksheet about the events leading up to World War I. When students can pair both importance and competence, though, motivation soars and students are much more engaged in the classroom.

Attributional Theory

The brainchild of Bernard Weiner (1985), the attributional theory of achievement motivation and emotion starts first with the perceived causes of achievement behavior. His theory puts forward the idea that the causes for achievement strivings can be laid at the feet of locus, stability, and controllability. Locus refers to the center of causality and seeks to discern if an event occurs because of an external or internal force. Stability describes whether the perceived cause is likely to be repeated (stable) or not (unstable). Controllability is used to further define a cause by whether or not it is in the control of the person in question.

If a student fails a vocabulary quiz, to what she attributes her failure will go a long way toward affecting her motivation for future activities. If she determines her poor grade is due to her not studying, she's attributing her performance to internal, unstable, and controllable factors since she could reasonably assume that, if she would have studied, she would have done better. If she blames her lack of success on a test that was intentionally designed to be frustrating and cause confusion, she's attributing her bad grade to external, uncontrollable factors because she didn't make the test and she doesn't know if the next test will be any easier.

While the former situation could expect increased motivation to study for the next test, the latter example would instead cause a decrease in motivation because of the attributions of her performance. Thus, students who ascribe their cause for success to internal, stable, and controllable factors have a higher degree of learning confidence resulting in greater motivation than those that see outside, unstable, and/or uncontrollable dimensions affecting their performance (Dickinson, 1995).

Control-Value Theory

This theory, most heavily researched by Reinhard Pekrun, integrates assumptions from the expectancy-value theory and the attributional theory in addition to theories of perceived control (Skinner, 1996) and models that include emotional considerations (Pekrun, 2006; Pekrun R., Goetz, Frenzel, Barchfeld, & Perry, 2011). This theory differs from the expectancy-value theory in the first element, control. Where expectancy in the expectancy-value theory simply considers if a student expects to be successful in a given task without ever looking too deeply at what causes those expectancies, control in the control-value theory integrates Weiner's attributional theory so that expectancies for success and the causes for those beliefs (attributions) work together to determine the amount of control one feels over an outcome. The second element of both the control-value and expectancy-value theories are very similar, identifying intrinsic and extrinsic values that combine for the overall value of the outcome (Pekrun, 2006).

The goal of this theory is to attempt to describe the causes of various emotions encountered in achievement settings. Both control and value work together to describe various emotions based on the positive or negate valuation of each component. For example, students might feel anticipatory joy for an activity that has a positive value and high internal control of success. Conversely, they may feel anger during a task that has negative value and an external control of failure. Boredom is encountered when there is no perceived value regardless of how high or low the control over the activity.

The control-value theory looks at the positive attraction or negative aversion of a task and whether the emotion activates or deactivates the learner's response (Pekrun R., Goetz, Daniels, Stupnisky, & Perry, 2010; Pekrun R., Goetz, Frenzel, Barchfeld, & Perry, 2011). For example, enjoyment is an activating positive emotion while contentment is a deactivating positive emotion. On the other side, anger is an activating negative emotion while hopelessness is a deactivating negative emotion. It is these emotions, categorized by control and value antecedents, that are thought to influence the role of achievement goals on academic performance (D'Mello & Graesser, 2012; Goetz, Pekrun, Hall, & Haag, 2006; Pekrun, Elliot, & Maier, 2009).

Flow Theory

Mihaly Csikszentmihalyi has conducted extensive research on a condition of optimal performance called *flow* (Shernoff, Csikszentmihalyi, Shneider, & Shernoff, 2003). This desirable work environment is a state of deep absorption in an activity that is perceived as intrinsically enjoyable. Flow is based on a symbiotic relationship between task challenge and individual skills. This balance is fragile, though, and imbalances can lead to negative emotional states such as anxiety if a task has a high challenge but the student has low skill, apathy for a low challenge with accompanying low skill, or relaxation for a high-skill, low-challenge task. Thus, flow occurs when concentration, enjoyment, and interest all converge in a task that is challenging but achievable based on perceived skill level. Breaking it down to a more granular level, flow is a fragile state of consciousness that coalesces when academic intensity (challenge and relevance positively correlated with concentration, attention, and interest) meets emotional response.

Goal Orientation Theory

Another angle with which to evaluate student behaviors and motivations are their learning goals, labeled performance and mastery by some (Dweck & Leggett, 1988), and ego involvement and task involvement by others (Nolen, 1988). Goal orientation describes how students either adopt a goal of learning for its own sake (i.e., mastery or task involvement) or a goal of achievement (i.e., performance or ego involvement) when involved in learning. The goals students adopt influence the quality, timing, and appropriateness of cognitive strategies used for the task. This in turn greatly impacts the quality of the student's overall achievement (Covington, 2000). Performance and mastery goals held by students have been found to be an outcome of the perceived goal orientation of the classroom itself (Ames & Archer, 1988).

Elliot and his colleagues, however, have subsequently postulated a three-tiered approach in which performance goals are divided into performance-approach and performance-avoidance (Elliot, 1999; Elliot, McGregor, & Gable, 1999; Linnenbrink, 2005; Nolen, 1988; Pekrun, Elliot, & Maier, 2009). Performance-approach goals are adopted when students desire to do well on a task and appear intelligent and capable, either to themselves, their classmates, and/or their teachers. Conversely, performance-avoidance goals motivate students to achieve because of a desire not to appear inadequate or unintelligent before others. Using this approach, not only mastery goals but performance-approach goals as well have been found to be beneficial motivational orientations for student performance (Elliot, 1999; Liem, Lau, & Nie, 2008).

Mindset Theory

No modern-day examination of student motivation and engagement would be complete without a close look at Carol Dweck's mindset theory. This theory first came about when observing students' reactions to failure and described two major patterns of cognitive-affect-behavior: maladaptive "helpless" responses and more adaptive "mastery-oriented" responses (Dweck & Leggett, 1988). The maladaptive pattern is characterized by challenge avoidance and low persistence when facing difficulty while the adaptive pattern is characterized by challenge-seeking persistence (Dweck, 1986).

Later, these approaches to one's ability were described by innate theories of intelligence. Students that held to an incremental theory of intelligence believe that intelligence is malleable and can be improved with effort. On the other hand, those that believe in an entity theory hold to the notion that intelligence or ability is fixed and cannot change regardless of desire or work ethic (Blackwell, Trzesniewski, & Dweck, 2007; Dweck & Leggett, 1988; Hong, Chiu, Dweck, Lin, & Wan, 1999).

Finally, these behaviors morphed into the modern descriptions of growth and fixed mindsets (Dweck C., 2006; Dweck C. S., 2008). The growth mindset is characterized by a belief that your basic qualities are things that you can cultivate through effort while the fixed mindset is focused on the understanding that you only have a certain amount of qualities, such as intelligence, skill, or morality, and nothing can be done to change those quantities. More than just a social-cognitive theory, the importance of having a growth mindset agrees with neuroscience research regarding brain plasticity (Mangels, Butterfield, Lamb, Good, & Dweck, 2006), the ability of the brain to rewire itself throughout one's life.

Self-Efficacy Theory

Most heavily researched by Albert Bandura (1993), self-efficacy theory proposes that beliefs about one's ability to produce a desired result influences how people think, feel, behave, and motivate themselves. Perceived self-efficacy impacts these areas through four major processes: cognitive, motivational, emotional, and selection processes. For the first process, cognitive, an incremental theory of intelligence is borrowed so that ability is seen not as a fixed quantity but as an improvable skill. One's self-efficacy beliefs about not only ability but the amount to which it can be increased will then greatly impact performance. Regarding motivation, Bandura borrows from other theories to describe three motivators: causal attributions (attribution theory), outcome expectancies (expectancy-value theory), and cognized goals (goal orientation theory). Thus, one's goal orientation, expectancy for success, and perceived causes for performance all work together to motivate students. Emotionally, the ability to cope is seen to affect avoidance behaviors and serves as the basis for actions in threatening or emotionally disabling situations. Finally, overall self-efficacy shapes the course of our lives by influencing our selection of activities and environments.

Cognitive-Evaluation Theory

First delineated by Richard Ryan and Edward Deci (Koestner, Ryan, & Bernieri, 1984; Reeve & Deci, 1996; Ryan & Grolnick, 1986), the cognitive-evaluation theory proposes that intrinsic motivation is based in the organismic needs for competence and self-determination. An event or environment will affect motivation depending on its functional significance, or interpretation of the meaning of the event or environment by the individual, being viewed as either controlling or informational. Controlling elements exist if an event or environment is experienced as pressure toward a specified outcome. This perceived control makes the person attribute the cause to an external locus of causality, thus making it controlled by external forces rather than internal desires. Informational elements, on the other hand, exist if an event or environment is viewed as providing relevant information for effecting change within an autonomy-supportive context. Students that believe an environment to be informational attribute causes to internal desires, thus facilitating an internal locus of causality. Functional significance, which determines self-determination perceptions, works together with perceived competence to fulfill a person's basic needs and affect motivation.

Self-Determination Theory

Subsequently put forward by Ryan and Deci, the self-determination theory is a macro-theory of human motivation (Niemiec & Ryan, 2009), applied to the narrower focus of student motivation, that puts forward the areas of competence, autonomy, and relatedness as the main areas of motivational causality (Deci, Vallerand, Pelletier, & Ryan, 1991; Ryan & Deci, 2000). As opposed to the aforementioned theories of student motivation which are largely based on social-cognitive constructs, self-determination weaves these social-cognitive needs (competence and autonomy) together with a larger need of the human condition: relatedness (Pintrich, 2003).

Building on the previously considered cognitive-evaluation theory, which put forth competence and self-determination as the major factors affecting motivation, self-determination theory renames self-determination as autonomy and includes relatedness, or relationships, as a third component that affects people's desires to engage or withdraw from activities. These three areas in turn greatly affect motivation, whether it be a lack of motivation or the formation of extrinsic or intrinsic motivation.

One of the contributions of the self-determination theory has been to examine four types of extrinsic motivation (external regulation, introjection, identification, and integration) and examine the positive characteristics of the latter two (Deci, Vallerand, Pelletier, & Ryan, 1991; Dickinson, 1995; Ryan & Deci, 2000). Specifically, extrinsic motivation that has a somewhat internal locus of causality, in which the learner finds value in the activity, is described as identified regulation. Likewise, extrinsic motivation with a perceived internal locus of causality, in which the learner synthesizes and adopts the values as his own, is described as integrated regulation. Both of these types of extrinsic motivation, in addition to truly intrinsic motivation, are known to increase autonomous engagement in activities and support higher academic performance (Deci, Vallerand, Pelletier, & Ryan, 1991; Niemiec & Ryan, 2009).

Person-Object-Theory of Interest

Postulated by Andreas Krapp (1999; 2006), this theory seeks to explain the development of interest and interest-related motivational orientations. Using aspects of self-determination theory, the person-object-theory of interest theorizes a two-tiered regulation system that consists of both cognitive-rational and emotional control mechanisms. It is within this regulation system that Krapp believes the three basic needs of self-determination theory (competence, autonomy, and relatedness) play a crucial role. Motivation is then characterized by its content or object specificity and will only occur if both cognitive-rational (competence, autonomy, and relatedness) and emotional feedback are experienced in a positive way (Krapp A., 1999; 2006).

Bringing it all together

As you can imagine, my head was swimming after diving into the deep end of over three decades of educational and psychological research into the field of student motivation. Who was I to decide between Dweck and Csikszentmihalyi? I understand and believe in Pekrun's interpretation of the expectancy-value model while at the same time Deci and Ryan's self-determination theory resonates with me and my experiences as a teacher.

Not wanting to genuflect at the altar of one researcher to the exclusion of all others, I began to look for commonalities between the various theories. The most glaring commonality was the idea of competence. Whatever name it goes by, whether expectancy in the expectancy-value theory, control in the control-value theory, competence in the self-determination theory, or self-efficacy in the self-efficacy theory, I found competence to be a central theme in most theories of motivation. Likewise, my own experiences showed me that students are more highly motivated to attempt and persevere in tasks when they believe that they have the ability (self-efficacy) to complete the task and can envision themselves (expectancy) doing it. Similarly, mindset theory begins upon the assumption that learning involves setbacks and works to describe the proper mindset needed to value the learning process in its entirety.

I also ran across the construct of value in most of the achievement motivation theories. Called value in both the expectancy-value model and the control-value model but described as cognitive-rational regulation in the person-object-theory of interest, I have seen how students' motivation is greatly impacted by the value a student places on a task or achievement goal. If the task is uninteresting or lacking in value, motivation will be hard to come by. Relating to both competence and value, the goal orientation theory (e.g., performance-avoidance vs. performance-approach vs. mastery) takes into account both a student's perceived competence and the inherent value of learning (or lack thereof) when describing how various goals affect motivation. Value is also considered as one of the three motivational processes affecting self-efficacy in the self-efficacy theory and a vital construct in flow theory.

However one views their impact and origin, emotions play a key role in motivational research. Pintrich's adaptation of the expectancy-value theory included an affective component (Pintrich & De Groot, 1990), emotional feedback is integral to the person-object-theory of interest, and the control-value theory is designed to try and explain the causal factors of achievement emotions. Whether emotions are caused by internal or external factors, a student's emotional state can greatly enhance or wreak havoc on learning (Pekrun, Elliot, & Maier, 2009) and enjoyment is essential to flow. Called the affective process in the self-efficacy theory, emotions are pivotal not only as an outcome of motivational processes but also as a conduit for those factors (Pekrun, Elliot, & Maier, 2009; Meyer & Turner, 2002).

Next, the idea of autonomy showed up not only in Weiner's (1985) attributional theory but as an aspect of control in the control-value theory, the key consideration in the cognitive-evaluation theory, and as a separate psychological need in the self-determination theory. Though not as cross-referenced as competence or value, autonomy has been found to be a great motivator in my experience as an educator, both as a teacher and as an administrator. Students, like most humans, desire to be in control of their lives and their day-to-day activity, even if that control is illusory. Incorporating choice into classroom activities has many beneficial effects (Dickinson, 1995) and autonomy is an important aspect of self-efficacy theory as it boosts involvement and persistence (Bandura, 1993) and flow theory since it is seen to foster a positive emotional response (Shernoff, Csikszentmihalyi, Shneider, & Shernoff, 2003). Without autonomy, intrinsic motivation withers on the vine since it is a result of an internal locus of causality (Deci, Nezlek, & Sheinman, 1981).

Finally, relationships, as a part of the relatedness aspect of the self-determination theory, brings into focus a quadrant that is absent from most motivational research: the social nature of people and an intrinsic desire to belong (Deci, Vallerand, Pelletier, & Ryan, 1991; Niemiec & Ryan, 2009; Ryan & Deci, 2000). Whether the connectedness is with a teacher, another student or a group of students, or with a school, students who feel like they fit in, like they are a part of something bigger than themselves, who feel that they connect with others, are much more engaged and motivated to learn.

In my extensive research into student motivation, I ran across a synthesis by Pintrich (2003) of social-cognitive constructs that attempts to cut through the clutter of most of the student motivation literature. Looking at social-cognitive-based theories, thus excluding the self-determination theory, he correlated the existing literature into five basic families or factors when describing student motivation: self-efficacy and competence, attributions and control beliefs, interest and intrinsic motivation, value, and goals.

My CRAVE acronym runs parallel with Pintrich's (2003) analysis in the three aspects of competence, autonomy, and value. What I term competence Pintrich described as self-efficacy and competence. Two distinct areas in his correlation, attributions and control beliefs along with interest and intrinsic motivation, are described by the single facet of autonomy within CRAVE. Similarly, his areas of value and goals are both described in CRAVE by the facet of value. One of the remaining areas of

CRAVE, relationships, incorporates the social aspect of students from the self-determination theory while emotions are somewhat more confused in the existing literature. Whether seen as antecedents or conduits of motivational behavior, they are a definite reality for students and have been often ignored by most social-cognitive theories (Pintrich, 2003).

CRAVE, then, can be used not only to explain student motivation but also as a diagnostic tool that I hope teachers can use to increase their teaching efficiency and the overall performance of their classroom. Students will be loath to learn if they lack sufficient motivation but how can teachers increase motivation if they can't identify its components? For some students, they lack interest in the learning activities because they see no value in what that are doing. Bringing in real-world applications can do wonders to increase motivation for those students but will do nothing for the negative impact of low self-efficacy. Teachers can make something as relevant as humanly possible but will still run into roadblocks if students do not believe they can accomplish the interesting task at hand. Other teachers will stumble because their students do not relate to them at all as a human and think that they are cold-hearted aliens bent on destroying the lives of young children. Similarly, student emotional states, sometimes not even having anything to do with the classroom, will derail student engagement. Who wants to learn about polynomials when their parents are going through a divorce?

Teachers are not educational psychologists by trade but are amateur psychologists by nature of their day-to-day activities. Tapping into student motivation is one key to successful instruction. After all, don't teachers wish that all students were intrinsically motivated to learn because they craved knowledge for its own sake?

The following table details how each facet of motivation relates to the major motivational theories in educational research.

Table 2: Motivational Theories Incorporated into the CRAVE Model

Strand	Key Motivational Question	Motivational Theories
Competence	Can I do this?	Expectancy-value theory; Attributional theory; Control-value theory; Self-determination theory; Goal orientation theory; Self-efficacy theory; Flow theory; Cognitive evaluation theory; Mindset theory
Relationships	Does this connect me to others?	Self-determination theory
Autonomy	Do I have to do this?	Attributional theory; Control-value theory; Self-determination theory; Flow theory; Cognitive evaluation theory
Value	Why am I doing this?	Expectancy-value theory; Control-value theory; Person-object-theory of interest; Goal orientation theory; Flow theory
Emotions	How do I feel about doing this?	Expectancy-value theory; Control-value theory; Person-object-theory of interest; Self-efficacy theory; Flow theory

References

Ames, C., & Archer, J. (1988). Achievement goals in the classroom: Students' learning strategies and motivational processes. *Journal of Educational Psychology, 80*(3), 260.

Bandura, A. (1993). Perceived self-efficacy in cognitive development and functioning. *Educational Psychologist, 28*(2), 117-148.

Blackwell, L. S., Trzesniewski, K. H., & Dweck, C. S. (2007). Implicit theories of intelligence predict achievement across an adolescent transition: A longitudinal study and an intervention. *Child Development, 78*(1), 246-263.

Covington, M. V. (2000). Goal theory, motivation, and school achievement: An integrative review. *Annual Review of Psychology, 51*(1), 171-200.

Deci, E. L., Nezlek, J., & Sheinman, L. (1981). Characteristics of the rewarder and intrinsic motivation of the rewardee. *Journal of*

Personality and Social Psychology, 40(1), 1.

Deci, E. L., Vallerand, R. J., Pelletier, L. G., & Ryan, R. M. (1991). Motivation and education: The self-determination perspective. *Educational Psychologist, 26*(3-4), 325-346.

Dickinson, L. (1995). Autonomy and motivation a literature review. *System, 23*(2), 165-174.

D'Mello, S., & Graesser, A. (2012). Dynamics of affective states during complex learning. *Learning and Instruction, 22*(2), 145-157.

Dweck, C. S. (1986). Motivational processes affecting learning. *American Psychologist, 41*(10), 1040.

Dweck, C. S., & Leggett, E. L. (1988). A social-cognitive approach to motivation and personality. *Psychological Review, 95*(2), 256.

Elliot, A. J. (1999). Approach and avoidance motivation and achievement goals. *Educational Psychologist, 34*(3), 169-189.

Elliot, A. J., McGregor, H. A., & Gable, S. (1999). Achievement Goals, Study Strategies, and Exam Performance: A Mediational Analysis. *Journal of Educational Psychology, 91*(3), 549.

Goetz, T., Pekrun, R., Hall, N., & Haag, L. (2006). Academic emotions from a social-cognitive perspective: Antecedents and domain specificity of students' affect in the context of Latin instruction. *British Journal of Educational Psychology, 76*(2), 289-308.

Hong, Y. Y., Chiu, C. Y., Dweck, C. S., Lin, D. M., & Wan, W. (1999). Implicit theories, attributions, and coping: A meaning system approach. *Journal of Personality and Social Psychology, 77*(3), 588.

Koestner, R., Ryan, R. M., & Bernieri, F. H. (1984). Setting limits on children's behavior: The differential effects of controlling vs. informational styles on intrinsic motivation and creativity.

Journal of Personality, 52(3), 233-248.

Krapp, A. (1999). Interest, motivation and learning: An educational-psychological perspective. *European Journal of Psychology and Education, 14*(1), 23-40.

Krapp, A. (2006). Basic needs and the development of interest and intrinsic motivational orientations. *Learning and Instruction, 15*(5), 381-395.

Liem, A. D., Lau, S., & Nie, Y. (2008). The role of self-efficacy, task value, and achievement goals in predicting learning strategies, task disengagement, peer relationship, and achievement outcome. *Contemporary Educational Psychology, 33*(4), 486-512.

Linnenbrink, E. A. (2005). The Dilemma of Performance-Approach Goals: The Use of Multiple Goal Contexts to Promote Students' Motivation and Learning. *Journal of Educational Psychology, 97*(2), 197.

Mangels, J. A., Butterfield, B., Lamb, J., Good, C., & Dweck, C. S. (2006). Why do beliefs about intelligence influence learning success? A social cognitive neuroscience model. *Social Cognitive and Affective Neuroscience, 1*(2), 75-86.

Meyer, D. K., & Turner, J. C. (2002). Discovering emotion in classroom motivation research. *Educational Psychologist, 37*(2), 107-114.

Niemiec, C. P., & Ryan, R. M. (2009). Autonomy, competence, and relatedness in the classroom Applying self-determination theory to educational practice. *Theory and Research in Education, 7*(2), 133-144.

Nolen, S. B. (1988). Reasons for studying: Motivational orientations and study strategies. *Cognition and Instruction, 5*(4), 269-287.

Pekrun, R. (2006). The control-value theory of achievement emotions: Assumptions, corollaries, and implications for educational research and practice. *Educational Psychology Review, 18*(4), 315-341.

Pekrun, R., Elliot, A. J., & Maier, M. A. (2009). Achievement goals and achievement emotions: Testing a model of their joint relations with academic performance. *Journal of Educational Psychology, 101*(1), 115.

Pintrich, P. R. (2003). A motivational science perspective on the role of student motivation in learning and teaching contexts. *Journal of Educational Psychology, 95*(4), 667.

Pintrich, P. R., & De Groot, E. V. (1990). Motivational and self-regulated learning components of classroom academic performance. *Journal of Educational Psychology, 82*(1), 33.

Reeve, J., & Deci, E. L. (1996). Elements of the competitive situation that affect intrinsic motivation. *Personality and Social Psychology Bulletin, 22*, 24-33.

Ryan, R. M., & Deci, E. L. (2000). Intrinsic and extrinsic motivations: Classic definitions and new directions. *Contemporary Educational Psychology, 25*(1), 54-67.

Ryan, R. M., & Grolnick, W. S. (1986). Origins and pawns in the classroom: Self-report and projective assessments of individual differences in children's perceptions. *Journal of Personality and Social Psychology, 50*(3), 550.

Shernoff, D. J., Csikszentmihalyi, M., Shneider, B., & Shernoff, E. S. (2003). Student engagement in high school classrooms from the perspective of flow theory. *School Psychology Quarterly, 18*(2), 158.

Skinner, E. A. (1996). A guide to constructs of control. *Journal of Personality and Social Psychology, 71*(3), 549.

Weiner, B. (1985). An attributional theory of achievement motivation and emotion. *Psychological Review, 92*(4), 548.

Wigfield, A., & Eccles, J. S. (1992). The development of achievement task values: A theoretical analysis. *Developmental Review, 12*(3), 265-310.

Wigfield, A., & Eccles, J. S. (2000). Expectancy–value theory of achievement motivation. *Contemporary Educational Psychology, 25*(1), 68-81.

Appendix 2: CRAVE Inventory

See aarondaffern.com/inventories for a printable version.

Answer each statement with either Strongly Disagree (SD), Disagree (D), Agree (A), or Strongly Agree (SA).

Competence

The student…

1. believes s/he can become smarter through hard work.
2. believes internal factors cause success or failure.
3. uses effective learning strategies.
4. expects to be successful when attempting a task.
5. demonstrates persistence in the face of difficulty.

Competence total: _____/20   SD = 1, D = 2, A = 3, SA = 4

Relationships

The student...

    6. maintains a positive relationship with the teacher.

    7. has a healthy and supportive social life with peers.

    8. enjoys working with others.

    9. has a positive self-image.

    10. is well-liked by others.

Relationships total: _____/20   SD = 1, D = 2, A = 3, SA = 4

Autonomy

The student...

    11. is intrinsically (internally) motivated to learn.

    12. prefers to choose his/her own tasks.

    13. dislikes being in a controlling environment.

    14. believes success is within his/her control.

    15. finds little value in tangible rewards.

Autonomy total: _____/20   SD = 1, D = 2, A = 3, SA = 4

Value

The student...

    16. enjoys learning for its own sake.

    17. only works hard on things s/he finds worthwhile.

    18. values learning new things.

    19. sees the usefulness in education.

    20. has a desire to perform well.

Value total: _____/20   SD = 1, D = 2, A = 3, SA = 4

Emotions

The student...

    21. is aware of his/her emotional state.

    22. is affected by mood swings.

    23. works more diligently when in a good mood.

    24. shuts down when having a bad day.

    25. can sustain long periods of attention on topics/tasks of interest.

Emotions total: _____/20   SD = 1, D = 2, A = 3, SA = 4

Appendix 3: Learning Style Inventory

See aarondaffern.com/inventories for a printable version.

Answer each statement with either Strongly Disagree (SD), Disagree (D), Agree (A), or Strongly Agree (SA).

Mastery

The student...

1. wants to learn useful information or procedures.
2. likes drills and teacher demonstrations.
3. learns effectively from lectures and practice sets.
4. has difficulty with open-ended questions.
5. enjoys feedback that is focused on improving performance.

Mastery total: _____/20   SD = 1, D = 2, A = 3, SA = 4

Understanding

The student...

6. wants to use logic and reasoning to solve problems.
7. likes debates and investigations.
8. learns effectively by being challenged and explaining his/her solutions.
9. has difficulty if too much emphasis placed on group learning.
10. enjoys asking, "Why?"

Understanding total: ____/20   SD = 1, D = 2, A = 3, SA = 4

Self-Expressive

The student...

11. wants to use his/her imagination.
12. likes creative activities and open-ended problems.
13. learns effectively by expressing his/her thinking in unique ways.
14. has difficulty with rote memorization and routine practice.
15. enjoys brainstorming and finding alternate solutions.

Self-expressive total: ____/20   SD = 1, D = 2, A = 3, SA = 4

Interpersonal

The student...

    16. wants to learn about things that affect people's lives.

    17. likes cooperative learning and role play.

    18. learns effectively by building a relationship with the teacher.

    19. has difficulty with independent work or unconnected content.

    20. enjoys discussions and groups experiences.

Interpersonal total: ____/20   SD = 1, D = 2, A = 3, SA = 4

ABOUT THE AUTHOR

Aaron lives in Ft. Worth, TX, with his wife Heather, his children Dave, Drew, Desiree, and Daniel. He is an avid disc golfer and sports nut, closely following the Rangers, Cowboys, and Mavericks. He enjoys fantasy novels, Star Trek: The Next Generation, the Marvel Cinematic Universe, and reading peer-reviewed educational psychology research articles.

Before becoming an education consultant, Aaron spent 11 years in the classroom as a 3rd, 4th, and 6th grade teacher. He also spent several years as a campus and district administrator of a charter school in Arlington, TX.

If you would like to learn more about one- and two-day training options for schools and districts, visit him online at AaronDaffern.com. You can also email him at aarondaffern@gmail.com.

www.ingramcontent.com/pod-product-compliance
Lightning Source LLC
Chambersburg PA
CBHW022007160426
43197CB00007B/317